For

William W. Greenough.

from his friend

A. T.

Boston. May. 1871.

Truly Yours &c. –
Justin Edwards

SAMUEL ELIOT.

BOSTON.
1869.

University Press: Welch, Bigelow, & Co.,
Cambridge.

TO

THE DESCENDANTS OF MY FATHER,

THIS SKETCH IS OFFERED,

IN THE HOPE THAT IT MAY EXCITE AN INTEREST IN HIS CHARACTER, RESPECT FOR HIS MEMORY, AND IMITATION OF HIS VIRTUES.

JUNE, 1869.

SAMUEL ELIOT.

1739–1820.

SAMUEL ELIOT.

MY recollections of my father are vivid and very interesting to me. I was nineteen years old when he left us; and, as time passes, and my measurement of character and conduct is better informed and enlarged, I look upon what he was and what he did with deeper value and respect. As numbers multiply about me, and individual character is more and more merged in their presence and their conventionalities, I feel a stronger respect for his excellences and for his peculiarities, — his strong sense and refined taste in literature, his sincere respect for religion, his vehement and generous feeling, his frank expression of his likes and dislikes, — all developed, governed, and made efficient, by his energy and right purpose.

I wish that I could place before his descendants a worthy sketch of his principles, his resolute adherence to them, and the animation and vigor that he put into every action. I should like to paint his manly, handsome person, and the activity of his movements, with the freshness and distinctness in which they live in my memory. I cannot satisfy myself in what I shall write, — it would be little to my credit if I did, — but I can record my recollections, and facts learned from others.

There were no startling or remarkable events in Mr. Eliot's life, but there was great progress in good things;

for his earnest desire for improvement, and his efforts to gain it, were constant and faithful. His life of eighty-one years included the teachings of poverty and wealth, the blessings of children and friends, and their loss, ambitions and loving hopes gratified and disappointed, perfect health, with much-prized independence of the services of others, and, in his closing years, almost entire dependence, from the loss of sight.

It is interesting and instructive to hear how success is achieved, and how prosperity and disappointment are borne.

Of my grandfather, Samuel Eliot,* I can give but few facts. According to a record left by one of the family, he was the son of Andrew Eliot, third in descent from the first emigrant of the name, from "the County of Summerset, England," who in "his will styled himself cordwainer." He was born September 17, 1713. He was a printer, publisher,† and bookseller; for in those primitive days, many trades and most of their mechanism often centred in one pair of hands. In May, 1735, he married Miss Elizabeth Marshall, of whom I know nothing before her marriage, but that she came from the West Indies.

Mr. Eliot's home and place of business was in a small

* A list of names and dates will be found at the end of the volume.

† In the autumn of 1743 a Periodical was published in Boston called "The American Magazine and Historical Chronicle, by Samuel Eliot, in Cornhill, and sold by Joshua Blanchard, in Dock Square, by Benjamin Franklin, in Philadelphia, and by others in New York, New Haven, and Newport." It was edited by Jeremy Gridley, Esq., and cost two dollars a year. It was continued three years and four months. — DRAKE's *History of Boston.*

The only relic of Mr. Eliot, my grandfather, as a publisher, that I know of, is a small volume that I have, entitled "A Display of God's Special Grace, in a familiar Dialogue between a Minister and a Gentleman of his Congregation. Printed by Rogers & Fowle, for S. Eliot, 1742." The author's name is not given.

house in Main, now Washington Street, between Court Street and the present Cornhill. There my father was born, August 25, 1739, and there my grandfather died, May 9, 1745, at the early age of thirty-two, leaving his widow with four young children, and without any means of support but what her own energy and capacity might procure.

They were very poor. Among the few incidents of his youth, that my father ever spoke of, was his having been obliged to run of errands in all weather, in thin clothing, and often ragged shoes. He attributed his subsequent vigorous health to this exposure, but his endurance simply proved a naturally fine constitution.

From a manuscript volume of Notes and Recollections, written by Dr. Ephraim Eliot, my father's cousin, I am allowed to copy some passages, and give the first here. This gentleman was a humorist and satirist.

"Mrs. Eliot, the mother of Samuel, was a proud woman, independent in her feelings, if not in her purse, and was possessed of a spirit which enabled her to bear up against the difficulties by which she was surrounded, and to prefer to rely upon her own exertions rather than the assistance of others, however well disposed her friends may have been towards her. But with four small children to provide for, she found it a hard task. From all accounts, the children were well disposed, active, and industrious, and as they grew up, did what they could for the comfort of the whole. Such was their destitute condition, that, Mr. Eliot has often related, he and his sister used to saw their mother's wood in the evening, and always felt happy when so employed. This state of poverty gave rise to a disposition to anxiety, of which he never could divest himself."

This, though not cordial, seems to me a high eulogy. A widow, at the age of thirty-one, burdened by sorrow, poverty, and care, had too true a dignity to live on bounty; and by steady energy and self-denial she educated her children to be active and respectable members of society, and had the wisdom and skill to make them happy, while they bore their portion of privation, and performed their share of labor. I do not know that a mother, in such a position, could do more or better.

I have heard it was said that my father, being an only son, was too much indulged; that he governed his mother and sisters, and acquired too much value for himself and his own opinions. The power that carried him cheerfully through deprivations in childhood, hard work and responsibility in youth and early manhood, may excusably have created much self-reliance; it was simply an overgrowth of what it was indispensable he should cultivate. As to governing his family, I think it could not have reached tyranny, for both mother and sisters had too much of the same qualities with himself to have submitted tamely. The indulgences within his mother's means must have been of very limited nature and number. Sawing wood in leisure hours seems to have been one of them.

There is little more to tell of this reserved and saddened lady. Four children survived their father, Elizabeth, Samuel, Ruth, and Sarah. Two sons had died in infancy. Truly she was acquainted with grief. Her last years were full of recompense in the characters and position of her children, and their faithful care of her comfort.

"The children," says Dr. Eliot, "were well disposed and industrious." They certainly were intelligent. Of Elizabeth, the oldest, two and a half years older than her brother, our Miss Hannah* said to me once, "She was very smart, and helped your Pa tend his shop as well as any man could." Ruth, two years younger than my father, was very bright-minded and witty, a little prone to satire. Sarah was born only four months before her father's death; her infancy was, therefore, shadowed by grief, and her youth burdened by privation.

The beneficent provision of free schools in Boston enabled my father, at the proper age, to attend the Latin School, under "Master Lovell's" teaching. "Master Lovell,"† famous through more than one generation, has now passed from memory, with the venerable brick school-house in School Street, where he taught, the name of the street being its only memento. I have heard (though not from my father) that Master Lovell flogged all the boys every Monday morning. He was certainly a stimulating teacher, and respected by his pupils; and Mr. Eliot's intelligence and ambition taught him the value of such instruction. Cousin Ephraim says: "Mr. Eliot used to value himself upon retaining the knowledge of the Greek language, which he acquired when a schoolboy. He read Homer while at the Grammar School, under Lovell, and relished it to the last. He was a self-educated man, all the advantages he ever received were obtained at the public school, but he acquired much

* Miss Hannah went to live in my father's house when she was eighteen, and continued in the family fifty years.

† John Lovell graduated at Harvard College 1728, made Principal of the South Grammar School 1738, was an excellent critic and classical scholar, a rigid disciplinarian, yet an agreeable companion and very humorous. In 1742 he delivered an oration in Faneuil Hall, on the death of Mr. Faneuil, an elegant composition. In the controversy between Great Britain and the Colonies Master Lovell took a very decided part. He joined the Loyalists, and left Boston March 17, 1776, and passed the rest of his days in Halifax. — *Abridged from* ELIOT's *Biographical Dictionary*.

learning; — had read much and conversed more with the literati."

The poverty that forced him to mechanical labor in the intervals of school hours, and to an early apprenticeship, limited the development of good powers, and the Doctor's phrase, "he acquired much learning," if meant literally, shows as narrow a standard. Mr. Eliot's desire for improvement, and the impossibility of gratifying it, excited a constantly increasing value for knowledge, and, in later years, a resolution that his children should possess, and, if possible, use faithfully, the best means of education accessible to them. His love of reading was always a source of happiness; books were to him the gems, the luxuries of life, to be earnestly sought, and carefully cherished. This taste, no doubt, grew in his earliest years; for his father's occupation must have made them the chief interest of the whole household. In those days (1735–40), books were rare treasures. In my own youth I remember such poverty and restriction in them, that I can hardly imagine there were any accessible to a boy sixty-five years earlier. Books, however, and periodicals my father did have, — borrowed, no doubt, — for I have six or seven extract books made by him before he was fifteen years old, filled with well-chosen selections from Pope, Addison, Shakespeare, Prior, and others, and from the Annual Register, Monthly Review, &c. There is much expression in these little manuscripts. The paper is coarse, but the writing is clear and elegant, and the careful paging and index prove a grateful sense of their value. When they met his eye in later days in his cosey little "Book-room," as it was modestly called, which held so many treasures, — the fruit of honest labor, — they must have stirred his heart like the face of a friend.

"At the suitable age," says the Chronicler, — "I do not know the year, — young Eliot was placed apprentice to Mr. Nathaniel Appleton, who was afterwards the first Commissioner of Loans for the United States. Mr. Appleton did business in a small, snug way, and was unable to do much for his apprentice, — nor was it then customary, — and much idle time was spent in the store. One day Mr. Amory, of the house of Jona. & John Amory, one of the first mercantile establishments in Boston, went into the store, and after some commonplace conversation said, 'Appleton, you have a smart boy here, and don't seem to have much for him to do. I wish you would let me have him. What will you take for his time?' He was a bounded apprentice, as was usual in those days, and he had the privilege of refusing an exchange of indentures if he chose. But the business was concluded so suddenly that he had no time to reflect, and on being asked if he would go with Mr. Amory, he said 'Yes,' took up his hat, and departed.

"'Now,' said Mr. Eliot to me, — 'now, Ephraim, it was the very best thing for me that ever did happen, but when I reached my destination, I burst into tears. I was a poor, fatherless boy, my mother a destitute widow, with three daughters, all dependent. From that moment, I adopted a detestation of the trading in human flesh which I have never gotten over, and hope I never shall. I had been literally sold by a master. Within a short time Mr. Amory gave me a guinea, and told me to buy some clothing he saw me in need of. I ran home and gave it to my mother to do with for herself and the others as she thought proper. Shortly after he gave me a piece of linen, which my mother distributed amongst us. Occasionally these things, or similar ones, were repeated, and though they were of trifling consequence to him, they were of vast importance to me.'

"In course of time Mr. Eliot became of age, and such was the confidence of the Messrs. Amory in his capacity and integrity, that, being desirous of devoting themselves wholly to the wholesale department, they consigned the retail business to his management, and he conducted it as partner for several years. He then assumed the business on his own account solely, and became a very noted shopkeeper, and for many years did as much or more business than any retailer in Boston."

It was in 1760 that my father came of age, and soon after, having hired of the Messrs. Amory their building in Dock Square, which included dwelling-house and store,* he established his mother and sisters there. Eight years of constant labor and faithful industry had raised the "ragged-shoed" boy to being merchant and householder. He had had no aid from any relative or friend excepting his employers; from boyhood his hours had been sobered by hard work and responsibility, and now care and self-denial were not diminished. The vigor of his nature is proved not only by his success, but by the energy with which he sought intellectual improvement, even while his labors increased. The mother's heart must have been brightened by such results of the integrity and capacity of her son.

* From a newspaper of the time I copy one of Mr. Eliot's advertisements : —

"Samuel Eliot,
At his Shop, near the Head of Dock
Square,
Has for sale,

Wool and Cotton Goods,
4 and 10 Nails,
China Bowls, &c.,
Men's Boot Soles,
Pistols, Powder, Ravensduck,
Metal Buttons,
Bibles and Testaments,
Kippers & Tillocks Snuff."

Mr. Eliot's nearest relative was his uncle, Doctor Andrew Eliot, the minister of the New North Church in Hanover Street. He was distinguished for talent and strong character, and stood high in the community, independently of the prestige then attached to his profession. He had eleven children, five of them sons, and having no resource but his salary, he could hardly aid a brother's son with anything but affection and advice. My father always cherished the deepest respect for his uncle, and passed every Sunday evening with him till his own marriage.

The apprentice having earned the honorable position of partner gave close attention to his enlarged duties. He used to tell us of the pains he took to serve every lady * that came to his shop; if one wanted but a yard of tape, he "waited upon her as if she were a duchess." He was fluent and highly complimentary to his customers, so that those who liked to laugh at him styled him "the Professor of Shop Oratory." In Dr. Eliot's manuscript his business rules are given, and two seem worth copying.

"When party politics prevailed, I expressed no approbation or disapprobation so as to involve myself in a dispute; a place of business is no place for disputation of any kind.

"Punctuality was always attended to in everything, to render the same advantages to every one, and to make people as punctual to me as I was to them."

The first statement records more self-command than will be generally estimated in our own days of strong party

* One day a lady, struck by the care and politeness with which he served her, said to him, "Mr. Eliot, if you treat all your customers as you have me, you will soon ride in your own coach." "If I ever have one, madam," he answered, "you shall be the first to ride in it." A promise literally fulfilled, as I was told by Mr. Jonathan Philips, who, in his youth, was an apprentice to Mr. Eliot for two years.

spirit. The years from 1760 to 1770 were full of anxious and alarming forebodings; deep excitement stirred every heart. Opposition to England was thought by a portion of the people not only absurd and unnatural, but wicked, and, having official support, they did not fear to express their contempt and disapprobation of it; while those who, from principle and conviction, maintained the rights of the people knew well what would be the bitter cost of resistance. Mr. Eliot's temperament was vehement, full of quick feeling and vivid interest, decided likings and dislikes, and he did not always restrain a too forcible expression of opinion. He felt the injustice to his native country in the recent acts of the Government; but besides the dread of ruin to his own prospects and hopes, if discontent became rebellion, — amongst his strongest feelings and established judgments dwelt admiration for England, her people, her ancient government, and her institutions. Loyalty to the beautiful island as "home" was cherished in many hearts that had beat only in America; and, sharing the feeling, this was to him a period of sharp and peculiar trial.

It was in 1764 that our Mother Government showed such ignorant courage in enforcing the Stamp Act, that fire-brand which kindled a slow fire unquenched for many years. In November, 1765, Mr. Eliot's "Master," as he always called him, Mr. John Amory, wrote to his correspondent in London: —

"If this Act is forced upon us we shall consider ourselves as slaves, without anything we can call our own. It must render disaffected to the English Government above a million of people, who, till now, were proud of being Englishmen, and as firmly attached to the interests of

England as if they had been born there. After being deprived of our natural liberties as men, and our privileges, granted to our ancestors by Royal Charter, we shall be very indifferent who are our foreign masters, and perhaps we may like them least whom we once liked the best."

One month later Mr. Amory wrote: —

"We cannot think the merchants who deal with America will find it their interest to increase their debt here by farther exportation, unless the Stamp Act be repealed. The resentment of the people here is at a high pitch, and will be much higher if not soon relieved. There will certainly be a combination of all sorts of people to throw off every kind of luxury in dress, which, you know, will take off two thirds of our imports from Great Britain. People begin to clothe themselves in our own manufactures. We are at present in a state of anarchy, but we are petitioning our Governor and Council that our Courts may be open, and this, we think, they must come into, as people seem determined to pay no taxes to Government if we are deprived of the benefit of it." *

These simple, strong words give a vivid impression of the prompt resoluteness of that early period, and two of the facts are very striking, — that two thirds of the importations at that time were for luxuries in dress, and that our manufactures were sufficient to be spoken of almost defiantly. When such things were written to a London correspondent, what must have been the amount of discussion and sympathy in homes, counting-houses, and offices, and what anxiety and sorrow, mingled with indignation and clear foresight of greater evils to come! Wealth, honor, pleasure, elegance, literature, clustered on that distant

* From a Letter-Book of the Messrs. Amory, kindly lent to me by James Amory, Esq.

shore, kindling imagination and ambition, and though this cynosure was not accessible to all, it had been a happiness to call it "Ours."

The intelligent activity and capacity which first attracted Mr. Amory's attention to my father, when a boy, and the honest earnestness that he gave to all he did, won for him much respect and trust, and secured to him a thorough knowledge of business. Evidently his character, industry, and skill brought a higher recompense than mere material success, for in 1765, when twenty-six years old, he married Miss Elizabeth Barrell, the oldest daughter of Mr. Joseph Barrell, then one of the wealthy and noted men of Boston. The family was a large one,—five sons and two daughters,—and they lived in a style of expense and freedom from control that formed a conspicuous contrast to the common family life of the period. The house, a large and handsome establishment, was in Summer Street, a garden and fish-pond * extended over what is now Franklin Street, and

* Mr. Barrell's fish-pond having been destroyed by lightning, his friend, Dr. John Clarke, sent him the following lines, which are given as a last century *jeu d'esprit.*

"What can I do? What can I say?
My pond, alas! has run away,
My gold and silver fish have fled,
And all my trout, alas! are dead.
Now will my Neighbour Clarke rejoice,
And raise his tantalizing voice;
And now a more provoking wife
Will jeer and vex me for her life;
My son, computing all the cost,
Will mourn twelve hundred dollars lost;
And Hannah, in a plaintive strain,
Will wish the water back again;
Hetty will act a generous part,
And sigh sincerely from her heart;

the whole was kept up with some degree of elegance. A few years later, thinking himself unreasonably taxed by the town fathers, Mr. Barrell left this beautiful estate in much indignation, bought another in Charlestown, and there gratified his love of show by building a finer house and laying out larger gardens and pleasure-grounds, adding greenhouses, and not omitting a fish-pond.* There he gathered his friends to admire his taste and success, to take fruit and coffee, and wander about the grounds. A vision of one such scene lives in my memory, but

But dear Eliza,[1] foe to sorrow,
Will keep her tears to shed to-morrow;
The Doctor,[2] like a generous friend,
Will hear my story to the end,
Then more than common sorrow feign,
And drink Madeira for his pain,
Happy to find that wine is plenty,
Though my deceitful pond be empty.

Ye streams, once more prolific flow,
And fill, O fill, the pond below!
Ye clouds, which overspread the sky,
Send down your treasures from on high;
To me your friendly stores impart,
But stay the all-destructive dart!
In answer to my fervent prayer,
Oh! give me Neighbor Russell's share,
And that I never may complain,
Oh! give me all my Parson's rain!
So will my little vessels ride
Upon my own domestic tide;
The fish, a new, imported race,
Again will find a dwelling-place.
Again bright Venus will appear,
As if she had been bathing here.
And I shall laugh at all who say,
'What time and money thrown away!'"

* This estate is now the Asylum for the Insane in Somerville, a part of old Charlestown. The name of Barrell is little known among us now.

1 Mrs. Eliot.

2 Dr. Bulfinch.

only a pencil like Watteau's could place it before the comprehension of others. The drive of two miles in the high English phaeton, with my father and mother, — the black coachman perched upon a small, round seat in front, — was a fitting introduction to the delights that followed. The house, with its spacious entrance-hall, its grand staircase, its many-panelled and stuccoed rooms, seemed a stately palace; and I walked, with my beautiful mother, through long alleys shaded by fine trees, with wide flower-beds on either hand, so radiant in color that one might almost have thought a rainbow had been thrown there. Groups of richly-dressed ladies and gentlemen moved slowly about, or lingered to feed the gold-fish or examine the greenhouses; the silks and laces, small-clothes, powdered heads, and three-cornered hats (it was the time of George III.) harmonizing well with the setness of form in the style of the garden. Seen through the vista of sixty years a glow still lingers on the scene.

It was a long step in the ascent of life when Mr. Eliot persuaded the brilliant Miss Barrell to leave the position of oldest daughter in such an establishment as her father's, (then in Summer Street) for a modest home over a shop in Dock Square, and the attendance of one young domestic; but I can well comprehend the vehemence with which he would seek to win her, and the attraction she found in him. He was full of youthful ardor* and intelligence, handsome

* It has amused me, while dwelling on what occurred a hundred years ago, to meet with these lines in a very modern poem, more appropriate, perhaps, than poetical: —

"His bearing, prospects, birth, — all these
Might well, with small suit, greatly please;

in person, with a decision and self-reliance that encourage trust, and are welcome to a woman when they are controlled by good manners and admiration of her.

My knowledge of Mrs. Eliot is slight; my impressions are more picturesque than distinct. All who could have described her were gone when I desired information except Miss Hannah, and she had not the power of analyzing or describing qualities or manners. Miss Hannah, that strong engine in our family movements for more than fifty years, went to live in my father's house in 1763, when she was eighteen years old, and for many years was the only domestic. She was observing and shrewd, of course living in close contact with her employers, and she retained till the end of a long life a fresh memory of the friends, events, and labors of her youth. She talked of Mrs. Eliot a little as one does of a winning child, — of her pretty looks and ways, of her love of frolic and practical jokes, of her impatience under illness or care. She told of her friendliness, — that she would call her to talk to her when solitude or languor was too heavy; and she described the delicacy of her organization and her variable spirits. The old lady spoke with emphasis and bated breath of

How greatly, when she saw arise
The reflex sweetness of her eyes
In his, and every breath defer
Humbly its bated life to her;
Whilst power and kindness of command,
Which women can no more withstand
Than we their grace, were still unquell'd,
And force and flattery both compell'd
Her softness." C. Patmore, *Faithful Forever.*

the many changes of her dress, — "more than your Ma and any three of you children ever used, dear," — of her "*ten white Holland aprons trimmed with lace*," and of her children having "*clean slips on every day*." The recollection seemed almost to bring back weariness and pain.

I gather, therefore, that Mrs. Eliot was pretty, animated, fascinating, winning affection easily, taxing it frequently, trying patience, and finding forgiveness as soon as she knew the need of it. My cousin the apothecary says, "She was a very lady-like woman, sensible and facetious." She had a kind heart, was quick to feel for others, and it is easy to imagine the power she would hold over such a temperament as Mr. Eliot's. It was a union of much affection, but its brightness was now and then shaded by variable spirits, sensitive nerves, and real sorrow from loss of children.

Mrs. Eliot's only sister, Ruth Barrell, was much younger than herself, and lived till 1820. She married Mr. John Andrews, a hardware merchant, and they both occupy a niche in my memory quite by themselves, and so distinctly, that I cannot help giving a slight sketch of what now seems so marked. Mrs. Andrews was peculiar in most things. Her figure was smaller, more delicate, than those about her; her feet and hands were small and prettily shaped; her complexion was fair and soft; her eyes were bright but small, her voice variable and low, and her enunciation so slow and measured that each word had a space to itself, so that one felt entitled to something better than common. Fortunately, some quickness of wit and repartee, with a flavor of sarcasm, kept up attention and interest.

This fairy-like figure was always dressed in rich silks of delicate hues, with much fine lace about the head and throat. It seems to me as if she was always seated in an arm-chair like a throne, with a footstool, and holding a fan or screen. I never recollect seeing her occupied with any woman's work, or hearing of her undertaking any, beyond a little drawing with pen and ink, a little versifying, or a little reading. But a wife, and mother of four children, must have been forced sometimes to real work; perhaps it was her skill and refined taste that kept it out of sight. Mrs. Andrews certainly had attractive powers and qualities, for my father and mother were much attached to her, and they estimated her by different though equally generous standards. Intercourse between the families was frequent; visits were often exchanged, beginning with dinner at three o'clock, and ending with supper at nine, after a rubber of whist. There was much fun, repartee, and animation, at these meetings, among the elders, I am, told (for this was before my time); but to the younger portion of the family they were more discipline than pleasure. Mrs. Andrews's badinage, and Miss Armstrong's sharp watchfulness and oppressive patronage, I recall as subjects of youthful dread.

Miss Armstrong was Mrs. Andrews's dame de compagnie, and became, I imagine, controller as well as companion. An entire contrast to Mrs. Andrews, she was, indeed, something fearful. Her figure was large, her movements were stiff and angular, her complexion red, her large, black, and piercing eyes always watchful and sharp, her voice deep and harsh. She always sat firmly upright, as if the comfort of joints was unknown to her, and the questions and remarks that came from her prim lips expressed an almost equally rigid judgment. She formed her standard of propriety and attraction from Mrs. Andrews's children, and whatever in my mother's differed from them, she appeared to consider unfortunate or wrong.

Mrs. Andrews, in her last years, had much sorrow, disappointment, and illness to endure, and it was all borne with meek and Christian patience. She found great comfort in my mother's gentle, cheerful companionship, and the simple, strong faith by which she lived.

Mr. Andrews was as peculiar in person and figure as was Mrs. Andrews. He, too, was small and erect in figure; his eyes were small and without expression, his voice thin, his enunciation slow and measured. His dress was always exact and uniform to a fold, from his first appearance in the morning, — his hair nicely powdered (but not crêped), with a tightly tied queue. A blue dress coat with gilt buttons, buff or straw-colored vest, delicately plaited shirt ruffles, and a radiantly white linen stock, laid in folds and fastened behind, black small-clothes, white silk stockings, with shoes and steel buckles, formed his costume in my early days. Later, he conformed a little to the changing style, but he never gave up either powder or stock.

Mr. Andrews was a successful hardware merchant, lived simply and elegantly, and in his leisure hours superintended the cultivation of a garden that was a public benefaction. His pretty, white house stood in the midst of it, shaded by fine trees, its front towards Winter Street, its back towards what is now Hamilton Place. The whole square (except what was occupied by the house) formed by Hamilton Place, Tremont Street, Winter Street, and the land now covered by a large stone warehouse, was radiant through spring, summer, and autumn, with a succession of bulbs, flowers, and flowering shrubs, chosen and arranged with the best taste and most loving care. It was enclosed by a wooden rail-fence, and gave cheering and delight to the passing citizens, who lingered as they passed.

The interior of the house showed the same refined taste that reigned without. A bow-windowed sitting-room, looking out under the shadow of a graceful elm upon the jewelled garden, was a lovely ladies' bower, with its soft carpet of light hues, pretty curtains, and cushioned window-seats; its panelled walls, low ceiling, and stucco ornaments; its white and gilded fauteuils and footstools; its painted screens, China figures, vases, and fanciful candlesticks. When the fairy lady, in full dress, was seated in it, with proper arrangement of chair, footstool, and screen, with a few friends about her, it was a pretty scene, particularly by the light of wax candles. When Mr. Andrews sold this charming estate, he built a house in Jamaica Plain,* and there arranged other gardens and grounds. During the siege of Boston, Mr. Andrews remained in Boston alone, and, in a series of almost daily letters addressed to his brother-in-law, Mr. William Barrell, of Philadelphia, gave a spirited and interesting sketch of the course of events, and the temper and condition of the people. It forms a quaint and spirited account of a period of intense excitement in the little town, when brave Massachusetts opened a contest with what seemed

* Now owned and occupied by Mr. Moses Williams, wine-merchant, and not externally changed at all.

an overwhelming power, and endured the first sharp sufferings of the Revolution.*

Of Mrs. Eliot's brothers I have little to say. I have heard that the oldest, Mr. Joseph Barrell, was a coarse, showy person, annoying our sensitive mother by his loud laugh and voice, his free jokes and compliments, and the jovial, careless style of his establishment. He had a large family of sons, and one daughter, who married Mr. Benjamin Joy. Mrs. Joy possessed a tenderness of feeling and manner, a depth of religious principle and faith, and a winning excellence in action, that are as rare as they are precious and beautiful. My father and mother loved her very dearly, and to all of us she was an object of admiration and affection.

My father was married, as I have said, in 1765; and when he placed his young bride in his own hired house, I can imagine him radiant with content, hope, and a sense of well-earned success. What a charm and glow brightens happiness, when it is the result of personal effort, industry, and self-denial! His mother and sisters had been previously established in a house near Brattle Street Church, — another proof of worldly success and of good judgment.

The following year his second sister, Ruth, married Mr. Jeremy Belknap, a clergyman, then settled in Dover, New Hampshire, but afterwards the minister of Federal Street Church, in Boston. He had much talent and

* Printed by the Massachusetts Historical Society in its Proceedings.

learning, quick wit, and most genial, delightful character and manners. His History of New Hampshire has won for him a name and reputation. Dover was then a small town, at a serious distance from Boston, and to soften the almost absolute separation from all her friends, the youngest sister, Sally, accompanied Mrs. Belknap to her new home.

One year later, in 1767, the mother who had so nobly and successfully struggled with poverty and care died, fifty-three years old; and then Elizabeth, the oldest child, joined her sisters in Dover, and remained there several years. She died unmarried, in Boston, in 1777, aged forty. Sally died in Dover, 1771, twenty-six years old.*

Changes followed rapidly in my father's life at this time. Till he was twenty-six, his experience was simply an enlargement of responsibility and increase of work, and the one event, the establishment of his mother and sisters in Dock Square. Within two years from his marriage, he was the only member of that peaceful household remaining in Boston.

But a fresh treasure was given to him, — a little girl who, though she lived but a few weeks, must have developed new powers of love, faith, and resignation in her parents. Such gifts, fleeting to our measurement, would often be called durable, if their power over the heart and life could be recognized.

* Dr. Belknap, in a letter describing her state of mind in her last illness, says: "She was remarkably cautious of speaking ill of any, and loved the company of those best who never talked against their neighbors. She was full of benevolence, candor, and modesty, a dutiful daughter, an affectionate friend, especially to our dear children. She had no gayety in her natural temper, but was rather melancholy, of few words, and in the company of strangers quite reserved." A touching sketch of a short life, begun in sorrow and poverty, and closed at a distance from her mother and home!

Mr. Eliot had now separated his business wholly from the house of the Messrs. Amory, imported goods from England for himself, and soon became desirous to make personal acquaintance with his correspondents, enlarge their number, acquire information, and satisfy, in some degree, his longing to see that magic land, the source, in his judgment, of all great and good things. What consultations and anxious interest his decision to make the voyage must have occasioned in the small, intimate circle, in those days when a visit to England was a more formidable undertaking than in our days of constant rapid movement can be at all comprehended! One or two ships made two or three voyages to England in a year from all the New England coasts, — vessels prepared for lumber, fish, and *ashes!* and not at all for passengers. The captains were respectable, trustworthy men, who would run no risks to increase speed, and who probably lacked the skill to use short-lived advantages. The voyages averaged fifty days.

It was in the summer of 1769 that Mr. Eliot determined to sail in the Caernarvon, Captain Moore, from Portsmouth, New Hampshire, for London, the vessel being "loaded with masts, of the value of £3,000 sterling." The journey to Portsmouth, at that period, occupied two days, and no doubt would now be called sadly rough. Four friends went with him to keep up his spirits, — his brother-in-law, Mr. Andrews, his cousin, Sam. Eliot, and Messrs. Hunt and Loring. At Portsmouth he found two Mr. Barrells, brothers of Mrs. Eliot, and when he embarked, August 7, the party numbered fourteen, who saw him on board, and bade him God speed. He was evidently attractive to his own sex, and of a cordial, genial nature. I am often reminded, as I write, of my dear and brilliant brother William, finding in my memories of him and of my father the same resolute execution of what principle and judgment directed, the same quickness of observation, capacity, and feeling, the same impulsive, vehement interest, mingled with a refined taste, love of genial intercourse, and withal a decided dislike of opposition. How much of usefulness and of charm was lost when my brother died, at the age of thirty-six!

A man-of-war schooner attended the Caernarvon one day out, for what reason is not recorded. A note-book, begun when Mr. Eliot left Boston, gives some facts of each day of his absence, but no opinions or feelings, and very few descriptions of objects or people, — a reticence to be rather regretted, since his observation and sympathy were ready and acute, and any sketches of those days are curious now. It was a rough, uncomfortable voyage: for twenty-eight days storms and fogs pursued the ship, the wind being sometimes so violent that they were obliged to eat what they could get upon deck, — a lumber vessel being the most unfit to resist such weather. In spite of this most unpoetic, uninspiring condition, Mr. Eliot committed to the note-book a rhymed letter to his wife, of which I give a small portion: —

> "Not rattling winds, joined with old ocean's roar, —
> Scenes novel quite, since never viewed before,—
> Not the smooth surface of the glassy sea,
> Nor playful dolphins, move my thoughts from thee, —
> Thee, my Eliza, thee, their constant theme;
> Whether I wake by day or nightly dream,
> Whether we smoothly sail or roughly roll,
> Thy dearest image fills my constant soul."

He goes on, mingling pretty vehement political doctrines with complaints of loneliness, and then referring to the Colonies, "owing subjection to one common head, says: —

> "But mourn, my Muse! — that union now is broke,
> And Britain's sons have found the galling yoke;
> They who gave freedom to the world before
> Decree their children shall be free no more.
> Rouse, then, my friends, and form a noble band,
> Save for yourselves, oh! save your native land
> From slavery's fetters, and a tyrant's hand!"

This has the ring of rebellion, and would not help the young merchant if the note-book should meet the eyes of a Birmingham correspondent.

The 20th of August some fishing vessels were seen on the Banks, one of which being French, a boat was sent from the Caernarvon to purchase wine or brandy, if possible, and Mr. Eliot, with his usual activity, went with the mate and two sailors. He found, to his displeasure, that fishing was going on, though it was Sunday; but being told that if the men did not fish they would play cards, he forgave that offence to the day. This shopping expedition in mid-ocean was a failure, as no brandy or wine could be had. On the 3d of September, four or five vessels being in sight, a series of movements began, of which I will copy the account from the book: —

"At five o'clock our sails were thrown back, in order to wait for the ship to leeward, our captain being very desirous to speak a ship bound home,* in order to put a letter on board for insurance."

It was six o'clock before they could hail the vessel, and learn that it was the sloop of war Hound, Captain Burr, of fourteen or sixteen guns. It was too late to send a boat

* "Home," of course, meant England; the Hound, sailing faster than the lumber-loaded Caernarvon, would carry news to the owners.

to the Caernarvon; but, at Captain Moore's request, the commander of the Hound agreed to hang out a light. At eight o'clock next morning, the lieutenant of the Hound went on board Captain Moore's vessel, and took back the letter to the insurers, and an invitation from Mr. Eliot to Captain Burr and his officers to dine with him. He was also the bearer of "a present of a hog, a sheep, and two geese."

"Our invitation we knew was accepted by the boat being left out. At ten o'clock we shaved and dressed, and at one the captain, doctor, and purser came on board. We entertained them with a ham and boiled fowls, a roast turkey, and a pair of roast ducks, and all the liquors of the ship. Captain Burr appeared a man of humanity and politeness, Dr. Spence sensible and sober, the purser no great things. We spent a very pleasant afternoon, they staying to coffee, and at dusk returned with another sheep."

Truly ocean life was a little more leisurely in 1769 than in 1869. But hospitalities were not ended by this sociable visit. The Hound sends the Caernarvon a ten-gallon keg of brandy, the keg being returned full of rum, and with it an invitation to dinner was sent to the lieutenant for the next day, which was declined. The following day the vessels were so near to each other that their captains exchanged greetings, and the gentlemen of the Caernarvon were invited "to take a glass of wine" on board the Hound. This being accepted, the commander's six-oared barge took them to the sloop at three o'clock, and it is recorded that they "spent a pleasant afternoon," and that they "drank Claret, Madeira, Teneriffe, Angelica, Malmsey, Ratafia, and coffee." This sounds rather jolly, but the sloop is described as in a sadly dirty condition.

On the 10th of September, the thirty-fourth day out, the passengers were landed in a boat at Dover, there they took "a post-chaise and four, and reached London the next day at five o'clock." The note-book gives many particulars of the journey, — calls Dover Castle "a paltry fortification," says, "many handsome women in Dover," "took a meridian* at Dartford," "walked up Shuter's Hill, which commanded a fine prospect." Such a group of friends greeted him the first evening in the Great Babylon, at the New England Coffee House, that he must have escaped the weight of loneliness often felt on first arriving amongst its crowds. He mentions Mr. Boylston, Mr. Bromfield, Mr. John Gray, and Mr. Martin; and later in the evening, at his hotel, five other friends, whose names are not given, "came in from Sadler's Wells, and gave me a hearty welcome, while I was at supper."

The next evening, after a busy day, "took a coach, with Mr. Gilbert Harrison, Mr. Deblois, and Mr. Neal, to the Haymarket, and saw "The Minor" and "The Author." Mr. John Harrison and a Mr. Wilson joined us. Adjourned to the Queen's Arms, St. Paul's Churchyard, where supped, and to bed at one o'clock." The night following, the same gentlemen went with him to Foote's, where he saw "The Devil upon two Sticks" and "The Padlock," appropriately supped at the Devil Tavern, and on this evening two o'clock was bedtime! Truly, pretty well for a quiet Boston gentleman of thirty!

My father was now in the fullest development of manhood, his energies and capacities strongly stimulated. He had an overflowing spirit of enjoyment and a love of

* An uncertain measure of spirits, in those days sometimes called a "nooning."

social action that brightened the cordiality of others. His feelings were keen and warm: beauty and tenderness touched him easily; his admiration was often enthusiastic, sometimes extravagant, his dislikes very decided, occasionally too frankly expressed. With spirits unchecked by care or disappointment, he was undoubtedly at this period of his life attractive and attaching. He certainly won many warm and faithful friends in England.

I give here two letters that he carried with him: —

"*To Messrs. Wright and Gill, London.*

"BOSTON, July 21, 1769.

"This you will receive by the hands of our friend Mr. Eliot. Although he has himself had the pleasure of a correspondence with you, yet as we have a very particular regard for him, he having been brought up in our store, we could not let him go to England without recommending him to your notice. We can freely recommend him to you as a gentleman of whose integrity, industry, and capacity for business we have the highest esteem. He has been successful in his business, and has now raised himself (wholly by his own industry) a good stock to carry it on with."

"*From Rev. Dr. Andrew Eliot to Stephen Sayre, Esq., Banker, London.*

"BOSTON, August 3, 1769.

"DEAR SIR, — Your goodness will, I hope, excuse the liberty I take to recommend to your notice a kinsman bound to Great Britain, who is very near to me, and who, I doubt not, will recommend himself to your esteem. He is the only son of my deceased brother, and is a young gentleman of good sense, and of an exemplary conversation. Any notice you may take of him will lay me under very great obligations, though I have no claim to such a favor.

"If I had more time, I should give my thoughts on our political affairs. Your ministry act a very strange part; their measures will more and more alienate the Colonies, and bring on an event which neither side ought to desire — an independency — much sooner than it would otherwise take place. I wish, I long for a change of men, without which I despair of a change of measures. The purposed partial repeal will have but little effect to conciliate the Colonies. And yet I wish they might behave with prudence, if that event takes place. I would have them take what they can get, and not relax any measures which will be likely to procure more.

"I am glad our representatives have made choice of worthy Mr. De Berdt to be their agent. That gentleman has much more integrity and wisdom than some who make a great bluster, perhaps with a view to supplant him. He hath hitherto served us with great fidelity, and I have great confidence that he will omit nothing that can be done. 'T is with me a great thing that he is a man of sincere piety. Such an one may be depended on much more than those who act from no principle, but to raise themselves.

"May the God of heaven interpose, and save both the nation and her Colonies from ruin. I have great hopes that the prayers of those who have an interest at the Throne of Grace will at length prevail.

"I would again beg you to pardon the freedom used by, dear Sir,

"Your obedient, humble servant,

"ANDREW ELIOT."

It was a stormy and threatening period. Controversies and complaints were constantly exchanged between the two countries, and little Boston made herself conspicuous by her protestation and firmness. Miss De Berdt * wrote to Mr. Reed (a gentleman of Philadelphia, whom she afterwards married), from London, in 1769, "To be an American, or a friend of America, is a great disadvantage."

This was natural; for, in English judgment, we were rebellious, ignorant children, who must be taught our place by wholesome punishment, and stern contempt. It would seem to have been an ill-timed effort for a young American to ingratiate himself with sturdy, loyal manufacturers and merchants. American credit was at a low point, and when that did not fail, goods were to be chosen according to the state of feeling at home, or left unordered. The determination mentioned in Mr. Amory's letter (which I gave above), written in 1765, to "give up all luxuries in dress," and to "use home manufactures," poor as they must have then been, had no shade of hesitation or fickleness in it, and expressed a character and resolution that would carry it into execution. If, however, Mr. Eliot found coldness and distrust, there is no record of it. He avoided political discussion, and kept himself steadily to business. Early and heavy responsibility had taught him prudence and self-command.

The note-book gives no sketches of persons or places; it is simply a record of occupations, amusements, the kindness he received, the places he visited. I wish he had been

* An interesting memoir of Mrs. Reed (Miss De Berdt), by her grandson, William B. Reed, Esq., of Philadelphia (printed, but not published), gives a picture of a most lovely and strong character, with sketches and anecdotes of her time. A notice is also given of Mr. Sayre. This charming volume was printed in 1853; and it would be well for the community if such pictures of high character and enduring patriotism could be made public.

less brief in some of his memoranda. For instance, three days after he arrived in London: "September 14, went upon the Thames in the morning to see the* fire at Buxton & Enderby's, thence to the King's Bench, to visit Mr. Wilkes, with Messrs. Dickerson and Geyer, and we were received with the most cordial expressions of regard."

"September 20th. To the King's Bench, where dined with Mr. Wilkes; spent the evening at home, writing to Mrs. Eliot."

"26th. Went to the West End of the town, saw Mr. Pownal, and was kindly received."

A few particulars of these interviews might have been curious now. Mr. Wilkes, then in the midst of his resistance to the Government, was a special object of interest to Mr. Eliot.

He left London the 29th of September, on a business journey, going first to Nottingham, "where a Mrs. Roebuck, with whom Mr. Denison carried me to take tea, inquired if the English language was the general language of America. The country is in general highly cultivated, and I observe that their fields are ploughed in a serpentine line, coming to a point at one end, so that each division has the appearance of a cornucopia: — they are the reality, that the emblem." On his way to Glasgow, he merely dined at Edinburgh, and says, "The road very rough and bone-setting, being, as far as I could judge, a bad pavement in general. The houses, rather huts or hovels, were

* Looking into the Annual Register for 1769, I find that "Buxton & Enderby's" was an oil-warehouse, on Paul's Wharf, and that it was wholly burnt, with many houses, a large timber-yard, and two large lightermen. "During the fire the river seemed on fire by the oil that poured into it from the repository. The oil consumed is valued at £20,000." Many swans were destroyed. It was the "river on fire," the traveller went to see.

such as gave me great pain, many of them being only a pile of stones, without any cement, covered with sods or turf, without any apparent door, window, or chimney. It was impossible for me to avoid feeling grateful for my infinitely better situation."

At Glasgow he was made a burgess of the city, and the ceremony seems simple and quaint enough. After walking about the city, he called on some of the merchants to whom he had letters, and one of them expressed his regret that, as it was Saturday, they could not make him a burgess, because they probably could not find a magistrate. A little later they seem to have caught one, for "soon after my return to Mr. Brown's shop, I received a summons to Mr. Keeley's inn. Was there introduced to Mr. John Brown, a magistrate, and five other gentlemen. Madeira was called for, and whilst we were drinking, Mr. J. Brown presented me with my ticket of burgess, which was put into the corner of my hat.* I was then desired to sit down with my hat on, and my health was drunk as a burgess of the city of Glasgow." This meeting was between twelve and one o'clock, and in a very short time four bottles of Madeira were disposed of. My ticket was no expense to me, nor "was I suffered to bear my proportion of the tavern bill."

He invited the gentlemen to pass the evening with him, but they declined. Five other gentlemen did visit him, whose names he does not give; he ordered supper, and called freely for Madeira, which, judging from the capacity shown in the morning, was probably a liberal allowance, and found afterwards, to his consternation, that the visitors would not allow him to bear even a portion of the

* The "three-cornered hat" of the time, — always so elegant.

expenses of the evening, "saying it was their custom." These Scottish gentlemen were no niggards in drinking or paying, apparently. One feels a little curious to know what was the advantage to a stranger of being a Glasgow burgess, beyond drinking Madeira in the morning.

The next day he breakfasted with a Mr. and Mrs. Elliot, and went with them to the Wynd Kirk, and in the afternoon "walked to the back part of the town, to what is called the High Kirk or Cathedral, where are three places of worship, one so extreme dark and gloomy,* that it is impossible almost in the brightest day that the brightest sun ever furnished, to see your next seat-mate. A most dreadful place in every respect. Such a place, to sit out a long, solemn service in, would rather tend to produce despair than hope. . . . . There are some few good faces and genteel persons, but in general, I never saw so ill-dressed and ugly people. Had Milton lived in Scotland, we should never have heard of 'the human face divine.'"

Glasgow was pretty well lighted, but it is noticed that, "till within three years, lighting the lamps was not permitted on Sunday evenings."

Mr. Eliot's second visit to Edinburgh was as brief as his first, for, arriving at five P. M., he left at seven, for Newcastle, much disgusted with the little he saw, and the much that he *smelt*, closing his account with: "If Edinburgh is derived from the garden of Eden, that garden should have been a swamp, or much injustice is done to it." At Leeds, he attended one of Stevens's Lectures upon Heads,† and says: "The person and manners of Mr.

* The crypts, — where Osbaldistone met Rob Roy, — no doubt.

† A small volume lies before me, called Mirth and Song, with the following title-page:

Stevens graceful, and his lecture highly moral, and justly satirical. Have scarcely been more pleased with any publick entertainment. Sat by the much-talked-of Anti-Sejanus, — one James Scott, an Episcopalian preacher in this place."

At his own request, Mr. Eliot was introduced to Dr. Priestley, at Leeds, visited him several times, and met him at the houses of friends. "That he is very sensible is well known, and that he is polite and engaging in his manners is equally certain. He told me that he reverenced the Americans, and from his whole manner, and from a little pamphlet he gave me, it is evident he is heartily engaged in the American cause." Dr. Priestley told him that, for two or three years, he had only thirty to forty pounds a year.

In the news-room of the inn at Leeds, Mr. Eliot met, one evening, a Mr. Gray, son of a nobleman, and a Member of Parliament, who was inquisitive about America, and talked of Mr. Otis, Mr. Cushing, and others. "I quickly let him know that I came from Boston, and we entered upon the subject of our late conduct, many parts of which he blamed, and I defended. He told me he found me a warm Bostonian, and that he thought it likely I should defend any measures that might be pursued there." I believe it also, — so long certainly as he was with those who were complaining of his countrymen. Immediately after

"Lecture upon Heads, written by George Alexander Stevens, Esq., and the Courtship, with a collection of Approved Songs, Printed in Boston, for John Whiting, of Lancaster, 1804." The Lecture is divided into four parts, and appears to have resembled the entertainments that gave Mathews such reputation, and his audiences such enjoyment. There are directions, interspersed: "[here show the example]"; "[shows the heads]"; "[takes off that and shows the other]"; the third part "[discovers two ladies on the stage.]" He ridicules fine gentlemen and ladies, oratory, law, and manners, with anecdotes, and what is meant for sharp satire.

the account of this animated meeting, we come upon the prices of calimancoes and camblets, the demand for shaloons, the value of tammies and serges, and the sales of cloths on market-days. At Coventry he visited a manufactory of ribbons, where the figured were woven by hand, and twelve yards could be made in a day. "Of plain ribbons, woven by loom, ninety yards could be turned out in a day! Extreme curious and pretty."

Seeing, in this venerable Coventry, the image of a man with his head and part of his body thrust out of an upper window of a house, which was called "Peeping Tom," he gives the story of Godiva with the addition, that at the annual fair in the town a woman rides through the streets, covered only with the skin of a beast,* decorated with ribbons, and followed by a grand procession of the city officers!

At Boulton's establishment, in Birmingham, even then forming an attractive exhibition, Mr. Eliot met General Paoli, at that time an object of great interest and respect in England, as well as on the Continent, from the noble manner in which he had governed the island of Corsica, and defended it against the French for fourteen years. When it was at last subdued, in 1769, General Paoli took refuge in England, and died there in 1807. He is described as "about five feet ten inches high, — his countenance not indicating anything uncommon, — his dress, a suit of Parsons' gray, with a queue wig."

At Bath, the next stopping-place, he gives some statistical items. Mr. Eliot found there his London friends, Mr. and Mrs. Hayley, Mrs. Hayley being the sister of John

* When I first read this, it seemed to me incredible that, in civilized England, such a vulgar exhibition could have been kept up till 1769, but on inquiry I found it was continued till 1854, (and perhaps it still goes on,) the modern rose-colored stockinet taking the place of "the skin of a beast," so much more appropriate to the occasion.

Wilkes, the notorious radical of that day. They introduced him to the resorts and amusements of the city, which is noticed as "perhaps the most beautiful city in England." But he thought it a sadly expensive place. "Mr. Hayley's family, of six persons, costs him £150 for six weeks!" He visited Gainsborough's studio, and speaks of him as a capital portrait painter. "His whole lengths cost eighty or one hundred guineas. I saw a number of fine pieces." At the balls, "the minuet began at six o'clock; tea between eight and nine, in the ball-room; left at ten. Two days of Bath life were sufficient to tire me out."

At Oxford, he records, with great astonishment, that at the Arundel Museum he was told that "the King of Spain had offered £100,000 for four pieces of marble, of ordinary appearance, which contained the original treaty between the Greeks and Persians, after the battle of Marathon!" He saw also a small piece of marble, upon which a gentleman of the University had labored three months, and had at last discovered the nearly obliterated inscription to be the "agreement with workmen for building the Temple of Apollo at Delphos!" No wonder he was astonished. Where are these venerable stones now? Blenheim, Stowe, Lord Temple's gardens are concisely mentioned, and it is recorded that in the shady avenues of these gardens he saw "Lord Temple, Lord Lyttelton, and Mr. Glover, the author of Leonidas."

The six weeks' tour ended in London the 8th of November, and he closes a grateful paragraph on the comfort and safety of the journey of eleven hundred miles with the remark: "Nothing has been wanting but a friend, to render my tour pleasant and agreeable."

A fortnight in London was filled with business, and

intercourse with friends, and he was fortunate enough to see Garrick in "The Jubilee," and in "Much Ado about Nothing." At Drury Lane he saw "The Wonder, a Woman keeps a Secret," and "The Padlock," the King and Queen being present.

From the 22d of November to the 29th of December (1769), Mr. Eliot made sundry business excursions to Norwich, Sheffield, Margate, and Canterbury, giving tokens in his notes of quick and shrewd observation. At Norwich, he was amazed at "the extreme bad grammar even the best people are accustomed to speak in: 'He think, he do, he have, he believe.' They seem, by their conversation, to have a mortal aversion to the letter *s*. Their language is not only ungrammatical, but they clip the King's English, being very fond of abbreviations; 'brig' passes for 'bridge,' throughout the precinct."

In the intervals of these excursions, he enjoyed very thoroughly, without doubt, sight-seeing, dinners, teas, and suppers, at friends' houses, and at the coffee-house, after the theatre. One evening he took tea with Mr. Wilkes, where he met "Mr. Reynolds (Mr. Wilkes's attorney), and Mr. Allen, father of the young man who was shot in St. George's Fields," in the Gordon riots.

A visit to the House of Commons gave him a sight of the King's robing and unrobing, and a long list is given of the speakers he heard. Lord Clare, Sir George Saville, Sergeant Glynne, Colonel Barre, and Lord North are the best known names in the list.

On the 11th of March Mr. Eliot dined "with Governor

Pownall, meeting Dr. Franklin, Mr. Monk, Mr. Bayard, and Mr. Reed, of New York; sat down at five o'clock; left at seven. N. B. — The servant refused *5s. 3d.* which I offered him."

He heard Garrick recite his ode on Shakespeare, the crowd being so great that he got in only through the kindness of one of the box-keepers. Another evening he heard the "Messiah" performed, "and was very heartily fatigued. The singing of Mr. Tenducci very disagreeable to me, though greatly celebrated; he put me in mind of the terrible Italian Opera." He saw the apartments in St. James's Palace, and attended a service in its chapel, where were the King and the Dukes of Gloucester and Cumberland.

On the 5th of March he went to the House of Commons to hear a debate upon the Repeal of Duties, — a subject of the deepest interest to Americans. He was obliged to wait in the lobby from one o'clock to five before he could get in, and just after he was admitted, when Mr. Grenville rose to speak, an order was given to clear the house, — a vexatious disappointment, but his strong interest carried him back at eleven P. M., to learn that "tea was not included in the repeal, 204 against 142." The only opera Mr. Eliot heard, as far as I discover, was "The Olympiad," of which he says merely that, being soon tired of it, he went away.

Windsor, Eton, Hampton Court, Greenwich, were all visited, and rather full memoranda prove that he saw them observingly, though he says, "Thus four or five hours have been spent in viewing two palaces, which, to have seen properly, would have required four or five days." He remarks of "Anthony Verrio's" paintings at Hampton Court, that, "with the brilliancy of their coloring, their boldness must be remarked."

Here is a chance specimen of a London day. A part of the morning was spent at Mr. Spragg's counting-room, discussing buttons; then calls were made on three other merchants or manufacturers; dinner taken with ten gentlemen at the New England Coffee House. In the afternoon he saw Mr. Sayre, who invited him to go to Dover with him, to electioneer for Mr. Trevanion (which he declined to do); drank tea with one friend, supped with another, and yet "passed the evening at home." Friends were always with him, and dinners, teas, and suppers were enjoyed at their different homes, or in their company at coffee-houses. Mr. Harrison, Mr. Denison, Mr. Dickerson, Mr. and Mrs. Hayley, and others are constantly mentioned as with him in sight-seeing, at theatres, and on excursions. He knew the excellent Mr. De Berdt, but says nothing of his daughter, afterwards Mrs. Reed, of Philadelphia.

Mr. Eliot kept his attention closely fixed on the course of Government and the proceedings in Parliament, and once was called upon by a Mr. Taleham, who asked him to visit Sir George Osborne, to give information on American affairs. Mr. Denison received a similar invitation, but they both declined to go, as they were not accredited agents, and other gentlemen were. They learned afterwards that Sir George Osborne had nothing to do with the proposition. He was a nephew of Lord Halifax, who had just been made Lord Privy Seal.

Dining one day at Mr. Hayley's he was told that Mr. Sayre wished to meet him there that evening. He returned to supper, and "on Mr. Sayre's mentioning to me the publication of Veritas, and desiring information with regard to facts, I told him what I had written. He desired a sight of it, and, at his request, I left the original with him." I do not know what the writing was, as this is the only reference to it.

To my father's temperament and tastes, this sort of life must have been a source of keen enjoyment and very strong excitement. But there was enough in the state of affairs between the two countries to create great anxiety and require skilful management and constant watchfulness by the merchant as well as the statesman. All business arrangements were made with provisos: certain goods were to be shipped only in case the Stamp Act was repealed, or when the duties on tea, glass, and colors were removed; and the actual condition of matters was such that Mr. Eliot returned home without goods.

On the 14th of April, 1770, the young merchant took leave of his kind friends in London, with much content, if rhymes addressed to a wife may be believed. I give a short specimen: —

"To Albion's shores I bid a long adieu,
And fly with eager haste to love and you;
Soon do I hope to clasp in warm embrace
The fair, possess'd of every charm and grace.

"Happy the man possess'd of such a wife,
The joy, the comfort, and the balm of life!
In mutual love a bliss is very sure,
Which grandeur cannot give, nor wealth procure.

"If happiness we 'd find,
It must be sought for in an easy mind;
Man's wants are few, and grant those wants supplied
Useless becomes whate'er we hold beside.

"Yet wealth is still with frantic zeal pursued,
Falsely considered as the greatest good;
This truth, eternal, claims my constant thought,
True bliss in virtue with success is sought."

Friends were faithful to the last. Five gentlemen accompanied him on his way to the ship at Margate, five others joined him there, while two remained with him till the vessel sailed. The weather was rough, and they anchored in the Downs, which gave Mr. Eliot an opportunity to see Sandown and Deal Castles. He describes them as "ancient circular stone buildings." On the 19th the ship got fairly under way, and the last sight of England was the illumination of Deal "on the enlargement of Mr. Wilkes,"— a welcome sight no doubt to the traveller, whose admiration for the patriot was strong, and whose interest in him had been naturally increased by intimacy with his sister, Mrs. Hayley.

The voyage seems to have been rough and disagreeable. It was not enlivened, as the previous passage had been, by excursions to other vessels or by ocean dinner-parties; and from the constant record of "head-winds and tumbling seas," I am sure the cry of "Land!" on the 4th of June, must have been a joyful sound.

On Rowe's Wharf, the fiftieth day from Margate, he landed, and was welcomed by Mr. Barrell, Mr. Andrews, and two of his cousins Eliot; and with this the diary ends.

We can easily imagine the sense of rest and content that reigned in the modest home in Dock Square, in the first weeks of summer. Mr. Eliot had much to learn, much to communicate. Every one was both politician and partisan, and to get news of the state of affairs and the temper of people in London, from an intelligent and shrewd observer, —one who had every inducement to learn all he could, and many facilities for gaining accurate information, — was the object of a wide and eager desire. Mr. Eliot had been eight months in England, constantly with that class of men whose interest in the trade with America was strong enough to make them keep a strict watch upon the movements of Government in relation to the Colonies, while his acquaintance with Pownall, Wilkes, De Berdt, and others, gave him access to early and exact information. Eager questioners and listeners must have often gathered in shop and parlor.

Two letters, written the next year, are the only record I find of his thoughts at this anxious period, and therefore I copy them.

"*To Messrs. Thomas Harrison* and John Ansley, London.*

"Boston, June 18, 1771.

"Dear Sirs, — My return to America, without goods, afforded me more leisure than my future life may ever see, some part of which I frequently thought I should appropriate to the business of writing you, notwithstanding your engagement to write me soon after my departure from England. But, however unemployed, I was somehow or other diverted from the executing of my purpose. I am now, thank Heaven, again engaged in the active scenes of life, and my time totally taken up in the hurry of wholesale and retail, cheap for cash, — in opening goods, and writing letters. Nevertheless, I could not excuse myself from acknowledging the receipt of your favor, of March last, by

* I have no knowledge of the Harrison family, beyond the fact that there were three brothers, — John, Gilbert, and Thomas. Mr. Eliot's respect and attachment for them must have been very strong, for he named his second daughter for one of the Mrs. Harrisons, — I do not know which. A life-size, half-length portrait of Mr. Gilbert Harrison hung in Mr. Eliot's library.

the opportunity which the return of our worthy friend, Mr. Gilbert Harrison, affords.

"The happy hours I spent in your company, and the obliging civility I was treated with by you, made an impression on my mind which time will not efface. . . . . I observed what Mr. Ansley said respecting the Lord Mayor, whose imprisonment, together with Mr. Oliver's, would have been astonishing to us Americans, if anything could have been so that the present Ministry do. The commotions among the People, it was expected by many, would have brought matters to a crisis, either freeing the Nation from the encroachments which have been made upon its liberties, or depriving it of those privileges which the cursed spirit of slavery had not yet wrested from us.

"But it looks as if matters were returning into their former channels, and that no successful opposition is like to be made. If, after all the noise which has been heard on the occasion, nothing is gained, much better would it be if nothing had been said. It is a saying, founded on truth and experience, that a conquered Rebellion strengthens a Government, which may be applied to every struggle of a People with their rulers; if, after such struggle, they find they have gained nothing, the end is worse to them than the beginning, as their weakness is proved, and the Minister's power confirmed hereby. Never should a Nation engage in open violence against bad governors, till they are sure of success. Till that period arrives, they should bear every imposition in a sullen state of inaction.

"But I will talk no more of Politicks, which I am very thankful I have no business with. I had rather go on in a dog-trot, retailing tape and pins, lawns, cambricks, and Irish linens, than be put in any dirty office or post of

Government. I say dirty, because in these days there is no office or post but what is so; and I say dog-trot, as I do not expect to gallop to a fortune.

"Do write me, and let me know how matters and things are with you. Are you married, or have you disclaimed all connection with Hymen? Do you remember the Crown in Bow Lane? I positively would give ten guineas to pass an evening there. Alas! what signifies wishing? But I do not despair of seeing my well-beloved friends in England once more.

"Remember me very particularly to everybody in general, to Mr. Thomas Wilson in special, and believe me to be, with real affection,

"Your sincere Friend,

"S. Eliot."

"*To Mr. Thomas Mifflin, Philadelphia.*

"Boston, August 26, 1771.

"My dear Friend, — Had there been any prospect of assisting Mr. Okeley in the sale of his edition of Serranus, you should have heard from me fully on the subject long ere this; but I have met with discouragement from those to whom you directed me more particularly to apply. It has been seen by Master Lovell, of the South Grammar School, in this Town, and by my Uncle Eliot, who were both of opinion that it would by no means do to introduce it, when so many better authors were already in use. They were pleased with it, as a specimen of the learning and piety of the writer. Master Lovell noted particularly a version of the Lord's Prayer, with which he was much gratified. The book has been left, as you desired, with the President of Harvard College, whose sentiment of it is entirely coincident with the gentlemen's above mentioned.

". . . . You conclude in a very melancholy manner, predicting the continuance of American slavery, unless a war should effect our freedom. The appearances of war have blown over, and the prospect has been gradually growing more and more gloomy, as the Ministry are daily acquiring firmness and stability. But a truce to Politicks. Our situation is too bad to be dwelt upon.

"I should have advised you fully upon Dobel's affair, had not Mr. Barrell wrote you so largely thereon. I hope for the honour of our native Town that the matter has been cleared up, and that you do not suspect him to have been guilty of the villany that has been charged against him. We live in an age in which everything is to be feared from the baseness and roguery of many around us, and I believe a few years last past have furnished such instances of villanous conduct as will be a perpetual disgrace to the annals of Mankind.

". . . . I may not omit to tell you that Mrs. Eliot — who desires her best regards to Mrs. M. and yourself — has lately presented me with a fine boy, whose life is the object of my earnest wishes. From the sad experience I once had of the loss of a child, I dread the thought of another separation.

". . . . I am, with the warmest wishes for the happiness of Mrs. Mifflin,

"Your assured Friend,

"S. Eliot."

The little child, whose birth brought such tremulous joy, lived only long enough to give new teachings from happiness and sorrow. A heart-broken letter to Mrs. Harrison, written September 30, 1772, tells her of little Charles's death from measles, on the 30th of August, when he was fourteen months old: —

"Previous to the disorder which tore our darling from us, he appeared in better health and spirits than in the more early period of his life. But the pleasing prospect was soon removed, the measles appeared upon him, and he is no more! Pity us, Mrs. Harrison, for the hand of God hath touched us. Mrs. Eliot is bowed down with affliction. . . . . You have, enclosed, a few lines wrote by Phillis Wheatley. A former production of hers I sent you some time ago."

To Mr. Harrison my father wrote, that the death of this little boy made him feel that he had not till then known what sorrow was. The trouble that first teaches us that lesson breaks, as it were, into the citadel of life; the same defences never are ours again, — the breach is concealed by the multiplied movements of life, and its duties, that cluster about us to cheer and to strengthen; but whole heartedness is not again possible. To how many is this experience first taught by the death of children! These parents were again childless, and great was their grief.

For the next few years I know of no incidents or changes in the life in Dock Square. In public affairs, and in the feelings of the people, it was an agitated and momentous period; but as Mr. Eliot still kept aloof from action or discussion in politics, their influence was on his character, and not on his position. He had felt the sting of poverty, and a heavy weight of responsibility for others, too recently to allow anything, not strictly in the line of duty, to interrupt his steady course. I give a few letters written at this time.

"*To John Harrison, Esq., London.*

"BOSTON, December 11, 1773.

"DEAR SIR, — However unworthy I may appear of being honored with your correspondence, from my long silence, and other reasons, yet give me leave to assure you there are few persons in the world with whom I so earnestly wish to keep up a correspondence as with my good friend, Mr. John Harrison. You will, with great appearance of reason, reply, that my language and conduct are not of a piece. To which I would request your permission to answer, as an apology for my behavior, that the calls of business have been, this summer and fall, such as have demanded my peculiar attention, from the sickness and confinement of my oldest apprentice, now in the last and best year of his life. Having only two young lads with me, my whole soul has been occupied by Irish linens, lawns, and cambricks, of which articles, by the way, I did not import half enough. Every moment has been devoted to my shop, and (please tell Mr. Gilbert Harrison) to the store in Wilson's Lane.*

"Thus much by way of porch. Have I made it large enough to admit the great Mr. Eliot, retailer of tape and pins at his shop near the head of Dock Square, and wholesale dealer at his store in Wilson's Lane?

"I perfectly agree with you in the opinion, that the measure of the iniquities of Government is not yet full enough to justify a very forcible opposition. It is, nevertheless, incumbent on the People of England to watch with a jealous eye the motions of an arbitrary Ministry, who, it

* The wholesale department.

is most certain, are, from year to year, gaining ground on that Constitution which is the glory of human nature, as considered capable of government, and a state of society. What think you of Mr. Hutchinson's Letters, and the Resolutions of the Court thereon? And what do you say, my good Sir, to the measures of the Ministry, by which the merchants of London are deprived of an opportunity of putting three and a half per cent in their pockets, and that upon a very large sum? An exclusive right should rather be diminished than enlarged, as the free spirit of that noble Dame Commerce abhors all restraint, and can no more take up her abode in an arbitrary state than a Sydney or a Locke in an Asiatic Court.

"You see and hear enough of the proceedings of this Town on the arrival of the tea. It is not for me to approve or censure. I have been very moderate in politicks, — or rather, *I have not meddled with them at all.* I had rather be behind my counter than in the forum; but at the same time I ardently wish the preservation and continuance of the constitutional liberty of my country, and would do all in my power, in a proper way, to support it.

"I am glad to hear you have recovered from your late attack of the gout, and hope your health will be better established in future.

". . . . Will you oblige me with another letter? Do, Mr. Harrison, and believe me to be, with the most perfect respect and esteem,

"Your sincere Friend,

"S. Eliot."

"*To Mr. Nat. Harris, London.*

"BOSTON, December 11, 1773.

"MY VERY DEAR FRIEND, — You might very well judge that the tender feelings of human nature were never bestowed upon me, or that I had suffered a total privation of them, should I omit to acknowledge, by a very early opportunity, the receipt of your very pleasing epistle of the 20th July, — pleasing as a proof of that affectionate regard, of which I had many instances whilst in England. I shall never forget the friendship of the house of Smith, Harris, & Hatfield, much less the attachment which you, to my honor, was pleased to manifest.

". . . . When I mention sensibility and the tender feelings of our nature as blessings, I am well aware of being opposed in the sentiment by many of the stoical sons of Earth, who contend that the pleasures of quick perception are by no means equivalent to the pains we must bear therefrom. But those who are not endued with this sensibility can never be admitted as competent judges in this matter. Lee has somewhere said, 'There is a pleasure in madness that none but madmen feel.' I shall not undertake to discuss the merits of this position, but I think I may with modesty assert that 'those who are tremblingly alive all o'er' are in a state upon which the man of a callous mind cannot pass judgment, being disqualified by nature or his own fault. The pleasures of the former are such as the latter intermeddleth not with.

'Our joys and sorrows, sure, are near allied,
And thin partitions do their bounds divide.'

"Alas! My friend, the dance of joy and the tear of sorrow succeed each other with a swiftness equal to the flight of time. We can scarce finish, or even begin, a congratulation but we are arrested by a tale of woe! I will not dwell on the subject, and shall only say that these ideas strongly remind me of the excellent advice of a much-neglected though admirably fine writer; you anticipate me in naming St. Paul, whose language is: 'Rejoice as though ye rejoiced not, and weep as though ye wept not.'

"You mention our Governor [Hutchinson]. That gentleman, in the last Session of the General Court but one, forced upon them the discussion of a subject which should never have been brought into view. The question he very imprudently agitated was, 'Whether the Colonies were bound by Acts of Parliament?' Long were the Speeches and Messages of the Viceroy on the occasion, and lengthy the Answers and Replies of the House. You will not expect me to determine upon the merits of either. I very heartily wish that Prudence had been of his Privy Council, when he was judging of the propriety of touching upon such a point.

"Scarce were the ruffled spirits of the People a little composed, when fresh fuel for a new flame was produced in certain letters * returned from England, written by Mr.

* It is a familiar fact that Mr. Hutchinson, while Governor of the Massachusetts Colony, wrote to his Government urging alterations in the Charter and other most unpopular measures, and that these letters were obtained and printed by Dr. Franklin. In consequence, the people demanded the removal of Governor Hutchinson, which, though refused by the King and Council *nominally*, was soon yielded to, and General Gage was appointed in his place. Governor Hutchinson had a beautiful place on Milton Hill, and many years later told an American gentleman, who visited him in London, and found him in very low spirits, that he often wished himself back on his porch enjoying that lovely view.

In the matter of the tea, the East India Company had stated to the Government that, if they would remove the import duty of threepence a pound, the Company would pay sixpence on exportation; but this proposition was refused.

Hutchinson. But as these letters have appeared in your papers, you must be acquainted with their operation here. I shall say nothing further of them.

"Our troubles were not to end here. An infatuated Ministry, ever intent upon planning schemes of malevolence against the Colonies, finding the Tea Act evaded by the total disuse of British tea, in the Southern Colonies, at least, — very wisely took it into their heads to force it down our throats. They accordingly commissioned the India Company to export the baneful herb. Three hundred chests are arrived here; but believe not that the people will ever suffer it to be sold. We have heretofore unwisely imported tea into this port, upon which the hated duty has been paid, which furnishes those who are inimical to the movement to prevent the sale of the Company's tea with an argument against us. For, say they, it makes no difference to the community whether the duty is paid by the gentlemen to whom the importation is consigned, or by those who have hitherto been the importers of the article.

"There is some appearance of reason in this talk. But still there is a manifest difference between our importing and paying the duty of our own free will and accord, and having the Ministry force it thus upon us. Their language is, 'If you will not import it yourselves, we will take care you shall not be without it, and more especial care that the duty is collected on it.' Must not the veriest slave revolt at such treatment?

"These villanous politicks have left me little room, and I have many things yet to say to the friend I hold most dear. Mrs. Eliot thanks Mr. and Mrs. Harris for their kind invitation to England, and so do I. I cannot but hope I shall once more see my dear friends in that country. We join in the most fervent prayers for the health, happiness, and prosperity of you both.

"I am, with unalterable regard, my dear Mr. Harris,

"Your sincere Friend,

"S. Eliot."

"*To Mr. Tom Mifflin, Philadelphia.*

"Boston, March 28, 1774.

"Dear Tom,—You tell me I am angry, or I should have answered the letters you forwarded by Palfrey and Gorham. This, perhaps, is a conclusion not deducible fairly from my silence, since many circumstances might occur that might make it, if not impossible, at least inconvenient, to write. Permit me to say, without the impulse of any angry passion, that I should suppose you judged me to be out of temper from consciousness that I had sufficient reason, and in compliance with an Apostolic direction, 'Be ye angry.' Now, if St. Paul, who was, to say the least, a sensible man, thought it was necessary to direct us to be angry, I can have no doubt of the propriety, nay, necessity of it, upon certain miserable occurrences in this miserable world.

" . . . . I believe it has been said, 'Keep not company with an angry man,' the justice of which advice I would by no means controvert; but at the same time I trust I shall not discredit my judgment by saying that I will never choose for my companion one who is totally unsusceptible of the passion, if such an one is to be found. . . . .

"I am much obliged by the venison sent by Gorham,—as much, most certainly, as if it had come to hand in the best order, instead of not reaching me at all. I am also greatly indebted to you for the repeated trouble you have had with the wine. Your directions shall be strictly complied with in the management of it when landed.

"You have herewith Mr. Hancock's oration, which you may possibly like to see. That your happiness may be as lasting as your existence is the earnest wish of

"Your sincere Friend,

"S. Eliot."

"*To Mr. William Barrell.*

"Boston, July 18, 1774.

"Dear Billy, — I find by your letters to Mr. Andrews, as well as from those few I have received from you, that my infrequency of writing is not pleasing. I am sorry you should think you have any just cause of complaint, though your displeasure is in itself obliging, — which ought to increase my concern. But separate from the avocations of business, I do assure you, I have not only a dislike of writing, but very forcible reasons of a private nature induce my silence.

"At this time, however, it may be incumbent on me to give you some account of my conduct, as far as it relates to the publick. You are very sensible that my plan has been to lead a retired private life, unembarrassed with Politicks and the disputes of the day. But matters have proceeded so far with us, that it is become impossible to adhere to such a system. The villanous Port Bill,* and

* The Port Bill closed the harbor of Boston from all commerce. The other two Bills referred to are probably, one by which the appointment of all officers for the Colony was vested in the Crown, subverting the Charter; and one which provided that all capital offences committed in Massachusetts should be tried in some other Colony, or in

two other bills much more alarming, and the measures that have been taken here in consequence led me to step forth to publick view. What more immediately caused my engaging was a Solemn League and Covenant being proposed by our Committee of Correspondence, by which the People engaged to purchase no goods imported after the 31st August. The Covenant was an emendation from that which was originally fabricated, that struck at the sale of all goods after the 1st of October, *whenever received*, and put a final period to the sale, though no possible advantage could result therefrom. It is unnecessary for me to enlarge, as you will find the subject very amply handled in the papers enclosed.

"I would by no means have you imagine that I was prompted by a foolish fondness of appearing in a publick character, or that interest solely actuated and directed me on this occasion. Had I attended very closely to the latter principle, I had still remained inactive, since you will readily judge, that by endeavoring to stem the popular torrent, and opposing a committee who, with great pertinence, might take for their motto, *Nemo me impune lacessit*, I must run a great risque of popular odium, incompatible with my commercial hopes and prospects. This, you will see, has had little influence, and however prudent or otherwise, I could not restrain my indignation at the arbitrary and tyrannic proceedings of those who would have the world consider them as the patrons and advocates of liberty. My patriotism and zeal for constitutional freedom and consistency urged me to combat the most pernicious measure that could be conceived and executed.

England. Both these bills were passed in 1774, the Government seeming to ignore the fact that English blood ran in the veins, and that English spirit would stimulate the action of the Colonists.

"I determined, if possible, to deliver my sentiments in Town Meeting, in order to which I made minutes of what I purposed to say. The substance of these minutes being impressed on my mind, it was not necessary for me to have much recourse to them, and I found myself able to speak with tolerable firmness, and what was said was well enough received by the people. You have it in the paper marked No. 1. You will notice a protest against the conduct of the Committee, by which you will find that a Motion was made to censure and dismiss them. This Motion was very precipitately made by Mr. Gray, and it totally precluded what I wished might take place, — a suspension of the Covenant till the sentiment and determination of the Congress could be obtained. They were the proper body to agitate the important question of Non-Consumption, and to them it ought to have been referred. Notwithstanding I was against this Motion, yet as I had opposed the Committee, I was obliged to vote with those who made it. I say I was against the Motion, not because it was wrong in itself, but because it was impolitick, not being at all likely to obtain, and having a tendency to irritate, which I would wish to avoid as far as duty would permit.

". . . . I must guard against your supposing that my ideas are opposed to a Committee of Correspondence subsisting among us. Very far am I from the remotest wish of an entire dissolution.

". . . . I cannot conclude without assuring you (though I trust it is in a good degree unnecessary) that, as I have formerly made a great sacrifice of private interest to the freedom and liberty of my country, I am now equally disposed to do all in my power to promote the happiness of the People. I am animated with the most fervent regard to the Constitution of this Province, and I will engage with alacrity, and adhere with firmness and resolution, to any feasible plan to restore and perpetuate it to the latest posterity.

"Tell Mr. —— that I wrote him immediately after the receipt of the wine, sent in the spring. I hope he duly received it. Believe me to be

"Your sincere Friend,

"S. ELIOT.

"Note well, Billy, that my opposition has been confined to the Covenant, and not to a Non-Consumption Agreement. Let a Non-Consumption Agreement be adopted by the other Colonies, in conjunction with this, upon a proper basis, — if I do not acquiesce and heartily promote it, may I meet those censures I shall justly deserve."

"*To Mr. Mifflin, Philadelphia.*

"BOSTON, August 13th, 1774.

"DEAR TOM, — . . . . You observe that your silence has been occasioned by your total attention to Politicks, of which it appeared to you I had taken a solemn leave. I acknowledge the truth of your apprehension on this head. I have not thought the times such, and the situation of things with us, adapted to my small exertions. I have, nevertheless, stood ready to assist in any well-grounded and well-planned opposition to the arbitrary, tyrannical, and cruel measures of Government. I feel myself animated by a true abhorrence of slavery in every form; and consistency of character and conduct, which I hold a prime virtue (but in which we are generally shamefully defective), must lead me to oppose domestick as well as foreign tyranny.

"This brings me, as a Parson would say, directly to the point. You do not like the Protest. I am sorry for it, but I cannot see it in the light in which it appears to you, and I still judge it capable of the fullest vindication. I think I may safely declare, that I have not been very tenacious of my sentiments and opinions, but have been ready to adopt other principles, when convinced that my own deviated from the line of Truth. My mind is open to conviction, and I shall bless the friendly hand that shall show me my errors, and point to the path I ought to tread.

"I have mentioned consistency as a virtue. How came you, then, it may be inquired, to depart from your plan, and step forth as an opposer of a measure calculated to serve your country, to which you profess yourself a zealous friend? It was my zeal to promote the publick good. A Non-Consumption Agreement may at a proper period, and under reasonable terms and conditions, be expedient. But the time in which the Covenant was promulgated, and the conditions of it, were such as rendered it inadmissible, unless the surrender of liberty, the sacrifice of property, and everything justly dear to man, are desirable. When a measure of such pernicious tendency was proposed, and its execution pushed by means incompatible with the Constitution, to have remained a silent spectator, — to have remained behind the scenes, — would have rightly incurred the curses of the present and future generations. . . . .

"But why protest? *Cui bono?* The Covenant was at this time circulating in the Country, unadopted by many Towns. It became us, then, to manifest publickly our disapprobation, in the hope it might influence to a rejection where it had not already obtained. It might, at least, put the People upon consideration, — highly desirable in every circumstance of life. Measures rashly engaged in are not likely to be steadily adhered to, and those whose firmness may be expected are those who deliberate before they act. Deliberation, in this case, infallibly secured the People from engagements which ought not to take place.

"You mention the effect of the Protest at Westminster. I think it will have the happiest influence. When it is observed that opposition is made to a domestick plan, because it is repugnant to the rights, liberties, and privileges of the People, must it not lead them to conclude us consistent sons of Freedom? They may justly argue, that we do not oppose their arbitrary principles from a dislike of the Government of Great Britain, but from an inbred aversion to tyranny, and that we are determined to burst the slavish bonds of an American demagogue, as well as the fetters of a British despot. Must not the exhibition of such a spirit place us in the first rank of the votaries of liberty, and raise us to be esteemed zealous, firm, and steadfast in two cases? This, Tom, is by no means a high-strained deduction, but the result of reason and common sense. . . . .

"I hope I have said enough to convince you that I have not deserted the Whig interest, as some among you, it seems, have asserted. I trust you will think yourself authorized to contradict the aspersion, which I am obliged by your having done already. Heaven and my own heart absolve me from a wish inimical to the interests of this American world, and I solemnly declare, that as far as I know myself, I am disposed to engage in any measure calculated to relieve us from the subjugation which has taken place, and which is further endeavored against us. I will exert my every power to establish the Liberty and Constitution of my Country, referring to my former conduct for the reality, and proof, of my present professions.

"I thank you for your invitation, which the situation of things will not admit my complying with, and I have little expectation you will be able to make a journey here. Your political and commercial connections will, I fear, confine you to Philadelphia. Farewell.

"Believe me your sincere Friend,

"S. ELIOT."

"Pray observe that my arguments are confined to the Protest to which I put my name."

This "League and Covenant," which Mr. Eliot vigorously opposed, bound the subscribers "not to purchase or consume any imported goods after the 31st of August; to break off all commerce, trade, and dealing with any who did, and with any who imported goods; to renounce all intercourse and connection with any who refused to sign the Covenant, and to publish their names to the world." This sounds despotic and violent enough to have come from Lord North, instead of from those who were resisting just such tyranny, and opposition to it seemed natural and right; yet it appears that some persons supposed my father was leaning more towards the English Government than to his own.

"*To Mr. Nat. Harris, London.*

"BOSTON, August 15, 1774.

"DEAR SIR, — Your favour of the 20th March was received with peculiar satisfaction, as indeed were all those with which you have been pleased to furnish me. I am greatly obliged by the solicitude you express for me under the difficulties the Port Bill involves us in. I can truly say I have a great regard for your judgment, but I cannot join with you in thinking that shutting up our Harbor was the most lenient measure that could have been adopted. I would by no means have you imagine that the destruction of the tea was, in my opinion, a proper thing; far from it. But could no means have been devised that should have separated the innocent from the guilty? I acknowledge that in many instances it is very difficult to make a discrimination; but in the punishment we are now sustaining, has not the Minister run so fast as to lose sight of justice and equity?

"Among what People was it ever heard that conviction preceded trial? Has this Town been furnished with any opportunity of justifying its conduct? Or, admit the difficulty of complete justification, had we been allowed a hearing, many circumstances might have been produced to view that would have lessened the apparent criminality of our doings.

"This may also be applied to the two Acts lately arrived among us, which totally alter our Constitution secured to us by Charles. Perhaps no Acts of Parliament were ever so despotick and arbitrary in their principles, and so cruel in their operation. To deprive a whole People of their rights and privileges, which they claim as men, and to which they have an additional title in this Province by the faithful performance of a contract, is too much to be submitted to. From the appearance of things amongst us, there is no great probability they will have any force. The most resolute determination animates all ranks of men to prevent their taking effect. Several gentlemen have taken the oath as Councillors upon the new Establishment, who have become exceedingly obnoxious in consequence.

"This was the work of a few days last past, and, therefore, I cannot advise you of the reception they meet in the Towns to which they belong. Those of them who are resident here are abundantly secured by an army and navy, to whom I wish sincerely better employ. It is thought the Governor will call an Assembly in October, but I believe the House, whenever it shall meet, will refuse to do business with a Mandamus Council. A Jury may possibly be found in this Town who will not refuse to act agreeably to the new regulations, but in the country such men will not be easily procured. Had it not been for the Acts last mentioned, something might have been done towards opening the port.

"You may wish to know my situation. I still continue in this town, and my business, since the 1st of June, has been greater than I had reason to expect, miserably obstructed as we are. As this letter is filled with Politicks, just observe that what dwells in the heart is apt to flow from the pen. This by the way of apology. You cannot wonder at our concern. Our very existence depends on the controversies of the present moment.

"Mrs. Eliot joins me in acknowledging the kindness of your invitation, which we cordially wish we could accept. That cannot be. Be persuaded then to visit America, with Mrs. Harris in your hand. A hearty welcome is the most I can promise you.

"I wish you every happiness, and am, dear Sir,

"Your very sincere Friend,

"S. Eliot."

"*To Mr. John Harrison, London.*

"BOSTON, September 15, 1774.

"DEAR SIR, — I duly received your obliging favour of the 31st March, and, notwithstanding your apprehension that, as a Bostonian, I might not approve some expressions you make use of, yet give me leave to assure you that a real opposition to my sentiments, if conducted with decency, is rather pleasing than otherwise. Every man has an undoubted right to form his own opinions, and it has an appearance of honesty and sincerity to manifest a different way of thinking from those with whom we converse. I have no conception of a more disagreeable state than that in which we must conceal our religious and political notions with care and circumspection. The interests of truth must fall a sacrifice to such villanous observance of times and seasons.

"I should gladly excuse myself from touching upon Politicks, did I not suppose you anxious to know the circumstances in which we are. The shutting up of our Port was a measure of extreme severity, and the two subsequent Acts, totally altering our Constitution, were not dictated by Justice or Policy. I say Justice, as the punishing a whole People, without the least appearance of a trial, I cannot but consider as utterly subversive of the principles of the British Government, as well as repugnant to our rights as men; and I say Policy, as I think it very impolitic to adopt plans which it might have been foreseen could never be executed among those who are animated by as high a sense of liberty as perhaps human nature is capable of.

"You will observe that I do not mean to insinuate that our conduct, in every instance, has been such as I could wish. A complete justification I do not contend for. All that I expect or desire is to make you sensible, that we have been treated with a degree of rigour much beyond our deserts. And I am persuaded that the event will prove that it would have been much wiser to have proceeded upon a more moderate plan.

"I shall not undertake to give a detail of the steps that have been taken to prevent the execution of the late Acts, as the newspapers you will receive with this will furnish the fullest information.

"I have been greatly undetermined as to the expediency of having fall goods ever since the arrival of the fatal Port Bill, as you may have perceived from the letters your House has received from me. My difficulty has not arisen so much from the decline of my sales, as from the state in which it was likely we should be. Some matters which I formerly mentioned as likely to take place have actually come to pass, — such as the shutting up our Courts of Justice, &c. A Non-Consumption Agreement has been proposed here, and I think the Congress now sitting at Philadelphia will adopt it, or, in its stead, a Non-Importation. Some few are for trying the effect of the Congress before they meddle with the business; but it is certain the voice of the People is in favour of an immediate stoppage.

"I much wish that such prudent and wise measures may be adopted as may terminate in our deliverance from our present miserable condition, and such as may once more firmly unite Great Britain and America, — a union highly desirable for the interests of both countries.

"You will please to deliver a letter you have herewith to

Mr. Ray, and asking you to remember me to all your friends, your sister Harrison in special, to whom I shall soon write, I remain, dear Sir, your obliged

"Friend and Servant,

"S. E."

The winter following this troubled and threatening summer, 1774-75, was a mournful and anxious one to all in Boston. The interruption of trade gave sad leisure for watching the course of the Government in England and the temper of the people here; and my father's tendency to anxiety found strong excitement in the increasing aggravation and alienation. Amongst other measures that inflamed the righteous anger of the people, a bill for quartering soldiers in the houses of the citizens of Boston was passed by Parliament. If this insolent design had been put in execution, I think the home in Dock Square would have been instantly broken up.

Dr. Ephraim Eliot, in his short sketch, gives an anecdote that belongs to this time.

"For many years Mr. Eliot's family resided in this house (in Dock Square), every part of which was often crowded with goods, leaving scarcely room for sleeping. About the commencement of the Revolutionary War, the building was offered for sale, and he had the refusal of it. He was in great tribulation, and sought the advice of his uncle, Reverend Andrew Eliot, who advised him to buy it. 'But I cannot command the money to pay for it, Sir.' 'Well, you have goods; have you not?' 'Yes, Sir; but I am afraid to let people know it.' 'Well,' said Dr. Eliot, 'buy it for me, Sam, if you won't buy it for yourself, — at all events, buy it.' Sam chose to buy it for himself, and, as he afterwards said, paid for it with a mere armful of goods."

What an expression of trouble, irritation, and determination, in the feelings of the people, is conveyed by this fear of having it known that he had goods!

Public affairs rapidly approached a crisis. The prevailing deep indignation found voice at Lexington and Concord in the early spring, and from that time there could have been little comfort in Boston. We cannot estimate what it was to the patriotic opponents of unjust oppression to be in constant contact with rough and rude soldiers, and haughty officers, who probably thought these absurd and insolent rebels fit only to be treated like insubordinate school-boys. It is wonderful that conflicts like that in State Street did not often occur, and that they did not occur is one of the strong proofs of the manly self-control and wise foresight of our noble ancestors. They reserved strength and indignation for larger opportunities.

More troops were sent to Boston; a military guard was stationed on the Neck, — the only means of access to the town, except by ferries, —and two regiments were encamped upon the Common. What melancholy days for a small community of intelligent, resolute men and women, estimating well and valuing deeply their rights and liberties, and now realizing that violence would be used to bring them to obedience!

Mr. Eliot felt that it was indispensable to find a more safe and tranquil residence, at least, for some months. His inclinations and tastes would have carried him to England, where many friends found shelter; but, besides a half-estrangement from that hitherto much loved land, he had neither funds there, nor sufficient here, to incur the risk.

Halifax, as being the nearest outpost of England, supposed to be still in quiet submission, was therefore chosen as the refuge, and, the goods being carefully arranged and the house closed, Mr. and Mrs. Eliot, with Mrs. Eliot's sister, Mrs. Andrews, left Boston in the middle of May. Another note-book gives the following history: —

"Monday, May 15th, 1775. At five o'clock this afternoon, embarked, with Mrs. Eliot and Mrs. Andrews, on board the schooner Halifax, under protection of Captain Le Tooch and Captain Haynes. We put off from the wharf, and anchored just below the Preston man-of-war, where we remained the night.

"16th. At five o'clock this morning came to sail, and proceeded with little wind to Deer Island, from where we took three boat-loads of stones, in order to put our vessel in better trim, which was loaded too much astern. Went on shore here with Mr. Hill and Captain Haynes. Afterwards went to Stebbing's Island, and the island just above, but could procure no live stock, an article we were in quest of. About three o'clock came to sail, — wind at southeast, which brought on a tumbling sea, and great sickness among the ladies. Wind freshened in the evening, which increased the distress of the cabin passengers.

"17th. Rose at five o'clock, and found Mrs. Eliot and Mrs. Andrews very sick and very low, — Mrs. E.'s distress so great as to lead her ardently to desire to be set on shore at Marblehead, where about nine o'clock it was determined we should go, though we were almost up with Cape Anne. But the wind was still contrary, and Captain Le Tooch, desirous of meeting Mr. Graves, who sailed about an hour before us, decided to touch at Marblehead. I endeavored to persuade Mrs. E. to give up all thought of stopping here, but being apprehensive that she could not sustain the voyage, we landed at three, and put up at the house of Mr. Sanders, my own plan being to proceed to Halifax. But we had not been long ashore, before we were visited by Mr. Hooper, Mr. Balch, and Mr. Wheatley, who gave us such alarming accounts of publick affairs at the place we were bound to, that Mr. Hill and myself determined to stop here for the present, provided we could get out of the schooner a few of the many necessaries we had on board. Upon our return to the vessel, we found the wind fair, and it was with difficulty we could persuade Captain Le Tooch to stop a moment. Our earnest entreaties, however, prevailed, and in about an hour, we hoisted out our trunks, and a few other articles, amidst a scene of the most violent hurry, agitation, and confusion, and we relanded about eight o'clock. Thus ended this unfortunate expedition, which has been attended, from the beginning, by many disagreeable circumstances, and in conclusion we were obliged to leave considerable provisions, furniture, &c., to be carried on to Halifax. We were happy in one material point, in our short abode in the vessel,— the politeness and humanity of officers and men. Our company consisted of Mr. A. Hill and family, a son of Captain Gay, and several female passengers.

"19th. Employed the forenoon preparing and shipping the trunks, &c., for Newbury Port. Mr. Balch passed the evening with us.

"20th. Visited by Mr. Payne and wife, who came on purpose to see us, and tarried dinner with us."

On the 26th, being still at Marblehead, Mr. Eliot notes, that he went with his landlord in a chaise about the country, to procure some provisions for Dr. Andrew Eliot and Mr.

Andrews, who were shut up in Boston, where food was very scarce, the country people not being willing to carry supplies, partly, no doubt, from a patriotic unwillingness to aid the soldiers, and partly from a natural fear of annoyance from them.

They succeeded in procuring "a fine salmon, three fowls, a quarter of veal, and four pounds of butter," — not an immense supply for two households.

The people of Marblehead, when the vindictive Port Bill was inflicted upon Boston, with a generous spirit of sympathy and kindliness, offered to her merchants the free use of one of their wharves — an offer gratefully accepted.

The ship Minerva, Capt. Callahan,* was lying there, bound to London, waiting for her passengers, who were flying from the evil to come. I copy again from the note-book: —

"27 May, Marblehead. Up at five o'clock, went on board ship, returned at half-past eight. At nine Callahan is under sail, and they take their departure, with a fine easy gale at Southwest. The passengers are Mr. Green and lady, [Mrs. Eliot's uncle and aunt], Mr. John Amory † and lady, Mrs. Copley and three children, Mrs. Jackson, Mr. S. Quincy, Mr. Balch, Mr. D. Green, Mr. Sears, Mr. Meyrick, of the navy, and Mr. Isaac Smith. Thus, by the departure of the Minerva, a total period is put to all my hopes of visiting England at this time, which last week I thought I should have accomplished, and had gone so far as to have my trunks ready for the voyage. Disappoint-

* Capt. Callahan was the grandfather of Mr. Edward and Mr. Charles Perkins, and of Mrs. Henry Cleveland.

† Mr. Eliot's former "master."

ment is the lot of man, and has been peculiarly my fate of late. Upon the breaking up of the Halifax visit, Callahan still in the harbor, I thought myself secure. Perhaps it may be best I should tarry,* and I must endeavor to be patient, and be resigned to what I now consider a misfortune. Went to Salem, to engage a coach to take us to Newbury Port.

"Attende the preaching of Mr. Storey, and between meetings attempted to go on board the Lively, with Mr. John Gallison, to procure letters from London, by Captain Hill, who arrived this morning, but finding it disagreeable to the people,* desisted from the attempt."

On the 29th of May, the party went to Newburyport, and the next day to Haverhill, where Mr. Eliot determined to remain, and establish himself and the two ladies as boarders with Mr. John White. This was undoubtedly a dark and trying period in my father's life. He was disappointed in his hope of reaching a safe and distant refuge, responsible for the security and comfort of those who were very dear to him, uncertain how he should hereafter find the means of living, and fearfully anxious, not only for his friends, but for his country, now actually involved in conflict with a power which apparently might easily force it, not only to obedience, but to sad subjection. His energetic and impulsive temperament demanded action and variety, and now he was forced into utter quiet. He loved to be among men and their movements, and had little taste for rural pleasures. I can well believe that patience and content were virtues difficult to reach.

* In the margin, in a later handwriting, is added, "And so it was."

† What an expression this is of strict observance of the Sunday, when news from England was of such vital interest and importance!

The people were everywhere alarmed by reports of troops having been landed at Salem, and of engagements having taken place there and at Cambridge. Minute men were preparing to march from Bradford and Haverhill with great zeal and courage.

Early in June (having bought a horse and chaise) Mr. Eliot visited his sister, Mrs. Belknap, at Dover, and in July made an excursion to some mysterious "C." I suppose it was Cambridge, as he noted a few days before, that Mr. White had "gone to Cambridge to see the Provincials." He gives no account of his journey, nor does he in the whole book make any record of public events, or of any opinions or feelings on public affairs. With the exception of this excursion, the summer slipped away in a quiet and tranquillity, contrasting wonderfully with the whirlwind of passion, action, and danger that swept through a part of the country. A "drive with Mrs. Eliot round the pond," in the morning, another "with Mrs. Andrews in the afternoon," a friend or two at dinner, or to pass the night, a visit to Newbury or Hampton, formed the only variety in their lives. He frequently says, "visited" so and so, "and took coffee"; or, "Mr. and Mrs. —— called to see us, and took coffee." Now and then long walks are mentioned, with three or four gentlemen, with the addition, — "took punch together at twelve o'clock!"

I give two letters written this summer.

"*To Mr. Wm. Barrell.*

"HAVERHILL, July 24, 1775.

"DEAR BILLY, — . . . . . You see by the date of this letter, that I am now at Haverhill, where, for the present, I have fixed my residence. Haverhill is about thirty-two miles from Boston, as many from Cambridge, and an equal distance from Portsmouth, finely situated on the Merrimack River, from which the land rises by an easy ascent. The prospect in some parts of this place is perhaps equalled by few, and exceeded by none. By none in America, as far as my recollection reaches, and Bath can alone be put in competition with it. Were this town built with the symmetry, elegance, and beauty of Bath, I am not sure that it would not be preferred before it. We are lodged here as boarders, in the house of a Mr. John White, which is, without exception, the very best in this part of the country, and, considered in itself, is large, neat, and commodious. The furniture is in proportion to the building, and the family is kind and obliging, so that we are accommodated in the best manner, much beyond our expectations, almost beyond our wishes.

"But, after all, Haverhill is not Boston, and to those who have once been housekeepers, you will conceive it must be disagreeable to become inmates in the best family, in the best dwelling, in the best situation under Heaven. Another capital difficulty I have to sustain is the dreadful change from a scene of busy activity to total idleness. To increase my misfortunes, I have no books with me, having brought from home only ten or a dozen volumes, expecting a full supply at Halifax, where, no doubt, I should not have been disappointed. I was mistaken in saying another capital difficulty, those mentioned being neither of them capital, when compared with the afflictions and distresses we have been made to suffer. To give you their history would renew my sorrows, and cause you grief, since you could not fail to sympathize with those who may with truth be styled the children of adversity. You may have heard of the Jew Morris, teacher of Hebrew at Harvard College. This man observed, that no People upon Earth could with so great propriety sing the Psalms of David as the People of New England, since no People resembled the Israelites so much in their settlement and progress. I was always struck with the parallel, and when our dispersion took place, — that terrible dispersion, which has scattered us over the face of the Earth, — I thought it complete.

". . . . I forbear to say anything of our publick affairs, as my situation is extremely unfavorable. We have an infinity of reports, more than nine tenths of which are fabricated by ignorance and propagated by falsehood, so that I am brought to total incredulity. Some of the reports may be compared to a strong gust, or driving storm, as they inspire fear and scatter destruction, whilst their authors are full as senseless and unfeeling.

". . . . We have had no letters from Boston since the 16th June, the day preceding the Charlestown engagement. I wish most ardently to hear from Mr. Andrews, Dr. Eliot, and his two sons, who are still there. Dr. Eliot is one of the best of men; he was extremely solicitous to leave the Town, and would have rejoiced to have come out as early, or before I did, his wife, with most of the children, having left him. What detains him? may be asked. I can, to his honour, answer, a principle of duty to God and his people. The Town was left destitute of ministers, except two or three. Many of his congregation remained, and many of other churches attended his preaching, so that, full as his house used to be, it became much more crowded than before. These persons were urgent in their applications to him to tarry; and could he, in such circumstances, which peculiarly require the aids of religion,—could he leave them as sheep without a shepherd? No! he could not. He tarries, to his eternal praise; and may Heaven be praised that, degenerate as the times are, Dr. Eliot has furnished an instance of virtue which would do honour to the first ages of Christianity.

"We have many reports that great sickness prevails in Town. I am not much concerned on his account. I trust in God that he will be delivered from the pestilence that walketh in darkness, and from the destruction that wasteth at noonday.

"'Why drew Marseilles' Bishop purer breath,
When nature sicken'd, and each gale brought death?'

"Your sister Ruthy intends writing to you at this time; your sister Betsy sends her warmest love, and beseeching you to take me into a corner of your heart, I remain

"Your affectionate Friend,

"S. ELIOT."

"*To Mr. Robert Treat Paine.*

"HAVERHILL, July 25, 1775.

"MY DEAR SIR,—It was long ago observed that man is the child of adversity and the subject of affliction. The experience of every age has confirmed the remark, and we, the inhabitants of Boston (that once blest abode), can now, in the bitterness of our souls, subscribe to its truth. I mean not, however, by this beginning, to pour out my heart before you in unavailing complaints. No, sir, that would be unbecoming the spirit of a man, which may and ought to sustain its infirmities and sorrows. . . . .

"I will not now attempt a description of the difficulties

with which we have been obliged to struggle, but must excuse myself with the quotation of *Infandum, regina, jubes renovare dolorem*, and shall proceed to acquaint you that after having been thrown about as the sport of fortune, not knowing where to fix, we are at last settled in this place, and, by the greatest accident, have our abode in the house of Mr. Jonathan White, whose wife was Mrs. Le Baron, of whom I have heard you speak very favourably. We are elegantly and commodiously lodged, but the mean accommodations of the old house at the corner of Wilson's Lane would be preferred, not to this residence only, but to the royal apartments of Versailles also. However, notwithstanding the pressure of the times, we enjoy ourselves as well as we possibly can, and my spirits are greatly higher than my expectations were concerning them.

"Since my leaving the Town, I have purchased a horse and chaise, which, though not needful for me in Boston, where I was constantly engaged in business, yet I judged would be absolutely necessary in the country, especially as I expected to take many journeys. I have not hitherto journeyed much, not finding that relief which I fondly wished from it, under a temporary depression. Journeying does not answer the purpose of easing a troubled mind.

> "'Those who beyond seas would go will sadly find,
> They change their climate, not their mind.'

"I think I need make no apology to you, my preceptor* and friend, when I acknowledge that I feel, with strong emotion, the distresses of my dear, native Town, my beloved Country, my valued friends, and my worthless self.

* I have no knowledge why Mr. Eliot calls Mr. Paine his preceptor, or where he lived at this time.

He surely must be less or more than man who can remain unaffected in such circumstances as we are brought into; and I conceive it to be disgraceful to a philosophic or Christian character to attempt to wrap itself in a stoical apathy. This would be to counteract not only the highest and best precepts of our religion, but the law written upon our hearts. But enough of this.

"I have left my house in the hands of a careful tenant; your maps are put in my upper front chamber, where I have stored the most of my furniture, under lock and key. Your other things are in the situation they have long been in, and doubtless they will continue safe, unless general ruin (which God forbid) should take place.

"I had a letter from Mr. Belknap the other night, in which he acquaints me with my sister having fallen down cellar, that she had broken her arm in the fall, and displaced the bones of three of her fingers. My sister Betsy is at Dover with Mrs. Belknap. We have had no letters from Boston since the 16th June. Mr. Andrews is still there; so is Dr. Eliot, whose tarry must be ascribed to the very best principles. His conduct in this dreadful season has advanced his reputation. May Heaven preserve him!

"I beg you would divest yourself of every suspicion, and think of me as favorably as you can. I shall endeavor to my utmost to know and do my duty. Mrs. Eliot is obliged in a high degree by the concern you express for her; her best regards attend you. Believe me, with every grateful sentiment,

"Your much indebted Friend,

"S. Eliot."

"*To Mr. John Amory, London.*

"HAVERHILL, August 2, 1775.

"DEAR SIR, — At the time of your departure, I believe you are sensible, I suffered as great disappointment as could possibly happen to me. To be obliged to give up a plan I had long meditated, and which at last I had the fairest prospect of accomplishing, — you can better judge than I can describe my feelings.

"At a period when letters are almost universally open to publick inspection, the difficulty of corresponding with an absent friend is so great as to make me uneasy at the necessity I am sometimes under of writing. In common seasons it was by no means an agreeable employ, as I found it a business I was not fitted to perform in a manner satisfactory to myself.

"It gave me some consolation in the midst of my troubles to find the course of the winds such as was greatly favourable to your voyage. I trust you reached the place of your destination very speedily, and that your passage was attended with every circumstance that could make it comfortable, pleasant, and agreeable. The Monday after you left us, I took my leave of Marblehead for Newbury Port, and the very next day came to Haverhill in search of a habitation during our banishment from Boston, that ever blest abode. By the greatest accident I fell in with Mr. John White, whom you will recollect as your quondam customer, and a resident here. With him I engaged board, if I should determine upon this as the place in which I should choose to reside, and left him with the obtainment of a promise that he would hold himself disengaged for a week or ten days. . . . .

"Having reason to think this Town as free from danger, and as well accommodated, as any in this part of the Country, I removed hither. How much longer I shall tarry is at present, for some special reasons, extremely uncertain. Should we be obliged to change our quarters, I shall consider our coming here very unfortunate, as Mr. White's house is by far the best that is met with hereabouts, and, in itself considered, is large, neat, and convenient. . . . .

"I shall not attempt to give you the news of the day, little of which lasts longer than the gourd of Jonah; the morning, when it rises, finds them withered away. This must ever be the case when the people are in a similar situation; when their hopes and fears are alarmed they grasp at shadows, and catch at the phantoms of an ignorant or vitiated fancy.

"Mr. Paine continues where you left him, and though, in compliance with your request and my own inclinations, I have taken great pains to convince him of the badness of his station and the superiority of ours, he is deaf to my arguments, and inattentive to my invitations.

"I beg you would present my affectionate regards to Mrs. Amory, to Mr. and Mrs. Harrison, and, in one word, to all my friends.

"Believe me, with the most respectful and sincere regard, dear Sir,

"Your obliged,

"S. Eliot."

In October Mr. Eliot made an excursion to Amoskeag Falls, and his account of them reads so quaintly now, when we care only for the amount of cloths and dividends they produce, that I will copy it from the note-book.

"October 25, 1775. Set out this morning for Londonderry in company with Messrs. Harrod, John Barnard, Frazier, White, Bartlett, and Pulsifer. Dined at Derry, at Colonel Holland's, and tarried the night.

"26th. This morning took our departure for Amoskeag Falls (myself on a horse of Colonel Holland), where we arrived about twelve o'clock, and found the Falls equal to our expectations. The height of the Falls causes a great rapidity of current, a loud noise, and a vast foam and great spray, and forms an object of grandeur, which the water-works of art, I think, cannot by any means equal. What is the regular uniform play of a fountain to the passage of such immense quantities of water over such tremendous rocks? After having taken a full view, it was proposed by Mr. Robert McGregor, who keeps tavern here, that we should cross the river to an island which makes one side of this scene. This was performed in a canoe through a part of the river where was a great rippling from large rocks, and would have rendered our voyage very dangerous, but that the skill and ability of Mr. McGregor were fully adequate to the undertaking. It was with much difficulty and some hazard that we proceeded from one rock to another, but at length we completed our design, having then another good prospect, though not worth the fatigue and trouble of ferrying over."

In November my father took a part of Mr. White's house, and established himself as a housekeeper, finding comfort, no doubt, in the increased occupation, as well as independence.

On the 16th of the following January the birth of a daughter brought great joy to the small family of exiles;

but sentiment was as much banished from the records as politics, and so the event is concisely stated without remark.

As a specimen of the social style of living at Haverhill, where many other persons were forced to idleness, I will copy a few of the daily notes.

"January 1st, 1776. Messrs. John and Sam White with me at dinner. Mr. Appleton visits me in the evening.

"2d. Called on by Mr. Prince. Walk with McHard. Spend the evening with Mr. Sergeant at Mr. Cary's.

"4th. Dined at Mr. Bartlett's. Mr. Wadsworth spends the evening with us.

"5th. Rode with Mrs. E. Afterwards went to Carr's on Pulsifer's horse. Evening at club.

"6th. Mr. Harrod at dinner with us.

"7th, Sunday. Heard Mr. Williams in the morning, Mr. Guild* in the afternoon. Spent the evening at Mr. Osgood's, where, besides our usual company, we had Mr. Wright, of Hampton Falls.

"8th. At home till noon, when drank punch with Mr. Rogers, McHard, White, Osgood, Saltonstall. Spent the evening at Dr. Saltonstall's, where we had the same gentlemen, with the addition of A. Johonnot and N. Blodget.

"10th. This afternoon came in S. Eliot [his cousin] and P. Coffin, who lodged with us.

"11th. Called on this morning by Mr. Emerson, of York. About noon Mr. Coffin left us. In the afternoon walked to Russell's with S. Eliot, and J. White, where we met McHard, Osgood, Bartlett, S. White, Saltonstall, and Captain Mulliken, who had gone down on skates. Having

* Of all these companions and friends, I can give no account, except that the Mr. Guild who preached on the 7th was the father of my brother-in-law, Mr. Benj. Guild, that he was made tutor at Cambridge in 1776, and died in 1792.

drunk coffee, returned as we had set out. Spent the evening at Mr. Cary's with S. Eliot, Mr. Osgood, and Mr. White."

On the 17th of March, 1776, the British troops left Boston, and on the 19th, Mr. Eliot went there for two days. It would be interesting to know its condition and appearance after such sad experiences, but he mentions nothing more than his going and returning. On the 15th of April he restored Mrs. Andrews to her husband and home, but did not remove with his own household treasures till November, the prevalence of the small-pox in Boston being a sufficient reason for delay.

Whilst living in Haverhill, some debtor, eager to get rid of bad money, insisted that Mr. Eliot should take $700 due to him in the American paper money of the time. "It was a dreadful grievous thing to your Pa!" Miss Hannah said to me; "he did n't know what to do with it; but after a while he found some old people in Haverhill that wanted to sell their farm; he wanted to get rid of the money, and so they made a bargain." * He says nothing in the note-book of this purchase, but speaks of making fences and planting trees just before leaving Haverhill. For a few years he had some receipts from this investment, in the shape of "corn, cider, potatoes, cheese, and pork," which were first taken to Newburyport, and from thence, by water, to Boston.

* I give Miss Hannah's words, from notes I took one evening when questioning her about old times. When I stopped writing, to ask a question, she said naively, "Well, dear, don't mind me; I can talk when you 're done writing," — not dreaming that I was recording what she told me.

How much profit resulted from this speculation, and how it ended, is not known. Two letters remain, written this year.

"*To Robert Treat Paine, Esq.*

"HAVERHILL, June 12, 1776.

"MY VERY DEAR SIR, — Had I known you were wishing to hear from me, a letter should have been despatched by the first opportunity. Without such knowledge, you will admit a fear of breaking in upon your important avocations as a sufficient apology for my silence.

"Your very obliging favour of the 9th May was handed to me two days ago, and this additional testimony of your friendly remembrance, you will permit me to say, was as refreshing as cold water to a thirsty soul.

"The small-pox in Boston has hitherto prevented my removing there, being apprehensive of danger to a dear little girl with which Heaven has lately blessed us. The major part of my goods are left in the state and place in which I stored them. When they will be opened, I cannot now determine.

"Mr. Howard, I fear, is in a very disagreeable situation; I cannot learn any particulars respecting him. How fervently I join in your aspirations for the friendly sociability of peaceable life, is beyond my capacity to express. Shall we ever again enjoy those happy moments of domestick intercourse we have formerly known? Shall we ever again meet in the friendly circle where I found blended pleasure and improvement? In the multitude of such thoughts within me, I wish I could tell you that the comforts of Heaven delighted my soul; we certainly need support beyond the reach of reason or philosophy. But though it is

Sunday, I would not have you imagine I am going to preach, or, if I had any thought of it, that I should arrogantly begin with addressing you.

" . . . . I am charged to present the affectionate regards of my 'dear lady,' as you kindly style her, and earnestly hoping that I may live in your esteem and affection, I am,

"Your obliged and sincere Friend,

"S. ELIOT."

"*To Rev. Mr. John Eliot,*[*] *Dedham.*

"HAVERHILL, October 19, 1776.

"MY VERY DEAR SIR, — I am greatly at a loss for a proper exordium in an address to a gentleman of your eminence in the literary world, since notwithstanding those floods of eloquence that roll on my tongue, the ink that fills my pen may be better compared to a stagnant pool than to a running stream. This, however, in the present case, may be a fortunate circumstance, as the highest circumspection becomes necessary in writing to one of your critical scientifick ability. I know the candour of your mind, and have experienced the goodness of your heart; these, it may be alleged, are the highest encouragement to the utmost freedom, and ought to remove the diffidence which modesty must feel. But shall I take advantage of the benevolence you manifest to obtrude my essays, and engross that time you might so profitably improve in pre-

* Mr. Eliot's cousin, son of Dr. Andrew Eliot, then settled at Dedham. The parish was called the "Clapboard Tree Parish," probably from some Indian word. Another Dedham parish was called Tiott.

In person Mr. Eliot was small and unattractive; his voice was high-pitched and sharp; from extreme near-sightedness, as well as from shyness, he was sadly awkward; but his temper and whole character were saintly, and they were severely tested in his home. He was universally respected. His preaching was nevertheless terribly oppressive to youthful hearers.

paring and uttering your refined discourses to a listening world? . . . .

"A proof may possibly be required by the infidels of the day of the learning and eloquence of the Clapboard Tree Genii. To support our assertions by convictive evidence may be, in many instances, a task of no small difficulty, but how easy a business for me now! I have only to say they have chosen, and continued for a long time in their publick ministrations, that prodigy of science, that light of the age, and, consequently, the guide of the blind, — Mr. John Eliot; and the lips of the greatest Sceptick must be closed in eternal silence! O Dedham, how dost thou shine among the towns of New England! Thy profound sagacity and clear penetration must ever entitle thee to veneration and respect; since, no sooner did this gentleman emerge from the dust and cobwebs of a college room, ere he had well wiped from his lips the flavour of a college pie, thus early didst thou select him from the sons of Harvard to become thy pedagogue, committed to him the all-important task of educating thy happy offspring! And now hast thou raised him from the school to the Church! To distinguish and reward merit is one of the noblest exertions of human virtue, and it was impossible to give a stronger evidence of thy attachment to manly worth, since the elegance of Atterbury, the metaphor of Seed, the perspicuity of Sharp, and the reasoning of Foster, are all comprised in the compositions of the renowned Mr. John Eliot. . . . .

"'Greece had her Demosthenes, and Rome her Cicero'; remember, O Dedham! thou hast thy Johnny Eliot, and value him in proportion to his exalted worth.

"Thus much, my lad, for my sweet little ode, set to

music, and 'the copious rolling floods of my elocution.' Mrs. E. says you are 'a sensible, saucy fellow'; the latter I think a proper epithet to be bestowed upon you by

"Your sincere Friend,

"S. ELIOT."

The exile to Haverhill closed November 12, 1776, when the little family returned to Boston. Injury from war had been wholly escaped, for the household possessions were safe,* and the goods, which had not been touched, had, of course, become much more valuable. But Mr. Eliot thought himself a sufferer. Compared with some other portions of his life, the eighteen months of banishment from "blessed Boston" were heavy and trying, yet, measured by the experiences of others, they were bright and prosperous. He had most abundant reason, as events were developed, to be thankful that he did not go to England with Mr. Amory in the spring of 1775. That gentleman left his children, a wide circle of relatives, and a large business establishment in Boston. He remained in England as long as funds could be sent to him from home; but that became very difficult, and he went to Brussels, where he lived in a most restricted and uncomfortable condition till the close of the war. On coming back to this country, in June, he found the displeasure against such absentees so strong in Boston, that he and Mrs. Amory were obliged to remain in Providence till the next December,

* On the preceding 11th of March, 1776, General Howe, then in command at Boston, issued an order that all dry goods and clothing, not belonging to loyalists, should be seized and put on board the English vessels in the harbor, — an order at once willingly obeyed, but countermanded the next day.

when the indignant town authorities condescended to permit them to return. It was a strong teaching to those who had escaped such troubles.

Mr. Eliot was once more established in his home, the new treasure, little Fanny, then ten months old, adding fresh brightness to the house, and a new incitement to content and industry. Boston must then have looked sadly marked and marred by the reckless waste and injury from the violence of war and the passions of repulsed soldiers. The Old South Church had been used — misused — by the cavalry, our Common had been a camping-ground, the Neck barricaded, and disease and poverty had been the natural consequences.

The active life in Dock Square was renewed with double zest, for the goods so successfully stored were much needed, and as my Sibyl said, "sold mighty well." It was a period of great anxiety and of great privation, for though Boston was safe, the rest of the country was exposed to danger and suffering that extended their effects to the most quiet and secure places; and I can well believe that steady work in the shop and the nursery was the best recipe for cheerfulness to both Mr. and Mrs. Eliot. But many valued friends were about them, with sympathies deeply stirred by a common experience.

Beyond these natural inferences, I can say nothing of my father's life through the seven years from 1776 to 1783; neither notes nor letters remain. But in the last-mentioned year a great and heavy sorrow fell upon him, in the death of Mrs. Eliot on the 24th of May. It could hardly have been sudden or unexpected, since the disease was dropsy; but after eighteen years of strong affection, and acute sympathy in joy and sorrow, separation can never be less than a shock, nor can the sharpness of the suffering be measured by others.

Fanny was then seven, — old enough to grieve over her loneliness at certain hours, but blessedly ignorant of what the real loss of a mother is. I imagine she was more an anxiety than an amusement to her father, and his quiet hours must have been very sad.

Peace was concluded between England and the States in January, 1783. Private as well as public relations between the two countries were, of course, in great confusion and disorder, and Mr. Eliot, having much business to arrange, and being glad to seek relief from the desolation of his home, determined to go to England. Mr. Nathan Bond had just married the sister of Mr. Elisha Sigourney, one of the apprentices in Dock Square, and it was proposed to him to occupy Mr. Eliot's house in his absence, and provide for the comfort and safety of little Fanny, and her faithful attendant Hannah. This arrangement made, he sailed in July; but there was no journal kept of the voyage and visit, and only a few letters remain, expressing much sadness and a pressure of occupation, but giving no details. One anecdote which he used to tell, connected with this visit, gave the beginning of an acquaintance and lifelong correspondence. Before leaving home he had been greatly delighted by a novel, received amongst other books from London, called "The History of Miss Temple."*

* This novel that so pleased Mr. Eliot was printed in 1777, when English novels were rare, and though strongly in the Laura Matilda style, was a great advance in refinement upon the Fielding and Smollett representations of life. Few could read it now except as a burlesque, but its sentiment and glowing language, I suppose, were fascinating at

In London he learned that it was written by a Miss Rogers, and walking one day in Sheffield with a friend, Miss Rogers was pointed out to him just entering a shop. He immediately followed her, introduced himself, and told her of his great admiration of her work. She amiably and graciously accepted this suddenly expressed homage, and invited him to visit her at her mother's house, which, of course, he did; and it always pleased him to recall his enjoyment in these visits, and the friendship won by his honest impulsiveness. He described this first interview to Mrs. Andrews; but I have only the following account of his second visit to the lady.

"*To Mrs. Andrews, Boston.*

"WOLVERHAMPTON, October 22, 1783.

"MY DEAR RUTHY, —. . . . I mentioned having seen Miss Rogers at Sheffield. I drank tea with her two days after at her mother's at Dronfield, where I fell in most happily with a gentleman whom I knew for a moment when last in Sheffield. I have the vanity to believe that the casual meeting gave mutual joy. I have received from him since one of the most friendly letters that was ever penned, together with a billet and pretty copy of verses, addressed to me from Miss Rogers. You shall see and hear everything upon this subject, as well as what passed in repeated interviews with the very justly celebrated Miss Seward, the author of the 'Monody on Major André,' to whom I

that time. The authoress presented Mr. Eliot with a beautifully bound copy (which is now mine), with a most friendly inscription and some verses addressed to her by Mr. Aikin (Mrs. Barbauld's brother), copied by herself. Miss Rogers married a Dr. Stokes. She continued a friendly intercourse with Mr. Eliot through his life. The "five sheets" from Miss Seward mentioned in the following letter have not been preserved.

introduced myself by a billet addressed to her at Lichfield, where she lives. I need not particularize my reception after informing you that she spent great part of Sunday in filling five sheets of paper for me, partly with her own observations on Dr. Johnson, whom she knows well, — which I have reason to think were written for me, — and partly with some copies of sweet poetical compositions. You are the only person in America to whom I mention Miss Rogers and Miss Seward, and till I see my dear Ruthy, she will take no notice to any one of what I have said concerning them. . . . ."

A few letters written to Mr. Eliot in this year are interesting, not only from their own freshness and animation, which time cannot dim, but because they show the impression which his character produced upon his contemporaries, and they form a various and valuable representation. They also prove confidence in his judgment, capacity, and good feeling, for all sorts of applications were made, and trusts confided to him. English creditors were to be appeased; sufferers from martial law in America sought redress; new mercantile connections were wanted; young men seeking their fortunes were referred to him for advice and funds; while commissions for purchases were not spared. Eight years of war had accumulated many wants. A church needed bells; one friend wished a carriage, another a watch; some wrote for books; ladies asked for jewelry and caps; and one frugally requested that the dress she sent in his charge might be dyed! It appears, too, that, while purchasing for others, he did not fail to collect pretty and useful articles for Mrs. Andrews and little Fanny. I give a few of the merely friendly letters.*

From Judge N. P. Sergeant.†

"HAVERHILL, August 6, 1783.

"DEAR SIR, — I embrace this opportunity of writing by Captain Mansis. Cannot inform about your friends in Boston, as I have not been there since I saw you; expect to go there in about three weeks, when I intend to see your Fanny, and have a little chit-chat. I think there is no doubt but we shall find subjects enough to talk of. I feel already that I shall miss my old friend there.

"We have hitherto had an admirable season; the hay is short by reason of the early spring drought. The prices of American produce are coming fast to the old standard. Everything wears a promising aspect, but only people's passions are raised very high about the half-pay to the officers; a little time will bring them to see their own interests, and the necessity of keeping up national credit and character. My whole quota of what is granted to the officers and soldiers is but about thirty dollars. Who would not choose to pay that small sum to have our officers return pleased, their faces shining with joy, congratulating their Country on the security of its peace, liberty, and independence, rather than that they should return sour, morose, and cursing the ingratitude of their Country? Surely no Nation on earth was ever under greater obligations to an army than America.

"Nothing has prevented us from granting the necessary

* I give these letters the more willingly, because my venerable friend, Mr. James Savage, once told me that letters of this period are not numerous.

† Judge Sergeant was appointed Chief Justice of Massachusetts in 1789, and died at Haverhill in 1791, aged sixty.

supplies for the support of the national credit but the ungrateful opposition to the officers' allowance. I trust the Massachusetts credit will soon rise very high; but you know I have always been much more sanguine than you and many others about this matter, therefore make what allowance you please.

"There has been an infamous affront offered to Congress, which, probably, you have heard: a few soldiers came down and made prisoners of them for a short time; but I am happy to hear our members, especially the Northern ones, behaved with proper spirit. Congress have so far resented the pusillanimity and cowardice of the Pennsylvania Government as to remove from it, I hope never to return. Large privileges are offered them at Maryland and New York, who are trying to outbid.

"Thus far Politicks. I have two personal requests to make. My son has sailed with Captain Mansis, upon short warning. I could not furnish him with any venture that I thought would answer any purpose. I have had no opportunity to purchase bills for him. I have, therefore, knowing your goodness, ventured to draw a bill on you for seventy dollars in his favour. As soon as I go to Boston, I purpose to purchase bills to that amount, or more, and send to you, perhaps with some further requests. My second request is, that you would inquire for one Farmer Durkett, who lived eight or nine miles out of London, and get some Siberia wheat of him, or somebody thereabouts,— quantity, three or four bushels,—and ship it by Captain Mansis. Shall trouble you frequently with letters, in hopes to get some in answer. Wishing you health and prosperity, I subscribe myself

"Your affectionate Friend,

"NATHL. PEASLEE SERGEANT."

Among other important commissions intrusted to Mr. Eliot, was the arrangement for publishing Mr. Belknap's History of New Hampshire, then just completed. Mr. Belknap had written to Longman, in London, on the subject, but had not received an answer, and wrote thus to his brother-in-law: —

"If Longman should have written to me before your arrival, he will doubtless have a copy to show you, and you need not wait for an answer before you conclude the matter. If there be necessity for any formal contract or assignment, you may act as if you were the proprietor of the copy."

Most of the few letters from Dr. Belknap are wholly on this subject. I copy a paragraph upon general matters: —

"DOVER, N. H., August 22, 1783.

". . . . The political state of the Country is not materially changed in any respect since you left it. Congress are fixed at Princetown, and have the offer from New Jersey State of a territory of twenty miles square in any part of the Jerseys, to be solely under the jurisdiction of the United States, and of £30,000 currency to be at their disposal. The import and the officers' commutation are yet unadopted, and in ten States violently opposed; and I am afraid we shall never agree upon ways and means to pay our debts till we are forced to it by some Foreign Power. A few heavy ships, our creditors' allies, stationed off each harbour, would soon do it.

"Don't you remember in the beginning of the late Troubles we had, in some of the newspapers, a Serpent cut into twelve or thirteen pieces, and the motto was, 'Join or die'? That Serpent is still our emblem; the parts have been cemented with *blood*, but the texture of it is dissolved, — each State claims a sovereignty as absurdly as if each of those parts had claimed to be a Serpent. We are known abroad as a United Sovereignty, but we want to be known among ourselves as Independent Sovereignties, each one having a negative not only on the other, but on the whole of the rest. If thirteen wheels were fixed on one axis, the motion might be regular and uniform, but thirteen wheels on as many axes require a much greater force to put them in motion than the packthread energy of Congressional resolves, remonstrances, and exhortations, of which we have had so many, one of which is now presently to be examined and voted upon, — not in every State only, but in every Town-Meeting, — before it can be carried into execution. It is about the mode of valuation, or taxation, or something of that sort, an alteration in one of the Articles of Confederation; and if they are all to be altered in this manner, and we are to take our own time to do it in every town, you may guess what a sweet piece of work we shall make of it.

"As to our New Hampshire Constitution, it has undergone another amendment, and is now, a third time, — I believe a fourth, — sent out for approbation; and the Convention are to have (I think) an eighth session this fall, to receive the Report, and, if necessary, mend it, and send it back again. Don't you hope it will be a good one at last?

"My family are all in tolerable health. Ruthy desires her love, and the children their duty to you, and I am, dear Sir, with much gratitude and respect,

"Your very affectionate and obliged Friend,

"JERE. BELKNAP."

*From Rev. Dr. Simeon Howard.**

"Boston, October 8, 1783.

"Dear Sir, — Not many days after you sailed from Boston I had such an account of the vessel in which you went, from persons whom I thought knowing in such matters, as made me anxious for your safety. I have accordingly been impatient to hear of your arrival in Great Britain, and was therefore made happy to-day, when your honest friend, Mr. Greenough, congratulated me on your having been some time among your friends in London.

"My frequent visits to you for many years past must have led you to think that you were of some consequence to my happiness. But you did not, I dare say, conceive — for I assure you I did not — that your absence would have made such a blank in my enjoyments. Deprived of so many friends as I have been, — some fled to heaven, and some to distant parts of the earth, — I feel myself a very solitary being. That house in Dock Square whose hospitable doors have so often give me a friendly welcome, and where I have passed more agreeable hours than in any

* Dr. Howard was settled at the West Boston Church, on the same spot occupied by the present building, in 1767. Mr. Eliot always attended at this church, and deeply venerated and loved his pastor. Indeed, he was universally valued for piety, wisdom, and faithfulness. He died in 1804.

I remember his tall and dignified figure, his white hair, and gentle, benignant manner, and the long-continued grief for his loss.

I add here an extract from an otherwise uninteresting letter from a Mr. Thomas Walley to Mr. Eliot, dated October 30, 1783: —

"Our singing (about which you were so anxious) is again revived, and several of the first characters in the society sit with the singers, which I know will give you pleasure. When I have the happiness of seeing you, I will tell you how it was brought about."

Mr. Eliot sang psalm-tunes in a full, clear barytone voice, but I never knew, except through this letter, of his interest in the church-choir which, many years later, my brother William arranged and led with great taste and success.

other house in town except my own, now calls up the painful remembrance of departed joys, and suggests many gloomy ideas. Little Fanny, however, whom I sometimes call to see, never fails to please me by her sprightly and agreeable prattle. You hear, no doubt, from other hands of her continued health, — a favour the more to be valued, because many children among us have fallen into a decline after the measles. May Heaven preserve her to be a blessing to her father and an honour to her sex, a fair copy of everything amiable in your and my departed friend.

"What are your negotiators about in Europe? Why is the definitive treaty so long in coming? Is the work of peace to be left incomplete, and the dogs of war to be let loose again? Heaven forbid it! But I cannot enlarge, being obliged to close my letter immediately, and send it to Mr. Greenough, or I shall miss the opportunity of conveyance. I am, with much esteem and affection,

"Your Friend and Servant,

"SIMEON HOWARD."

*From Rev. Dr. Gordon.**

"JAMAICA PLAINS, December 8, 1783.

"And so, Sir, you thought — did you? — to prevent all further correspondence by not telling me how I was to direct to you? And could you believe me to be so

* Allen, in his Biographical Dictionary, says of Dr. Gordon, that "he was a strict Calvinist, *yet* he possessed a liberal mind and a very sociable disposition. He was even sometimes facetious," — a slight token of what Calvinists were in those days. Dr. Gordon was at this date settled in Roxbury. He left a parish in London in 1770, from interest in this country, but returned to England in 1786, to publish his History of the American War, and settled in a parish in Huntingdonshire. He died in 1807.

young, or so antiquated, that I could not trace you? This may convince you of the contrary.

"I am glad you are so well satisfied with my Portsmouth friends. The lieutenant and his wife are very grateful, and gratitude, you know, is ofttimes extravagant in its expressions; and therefore you must make some deductions for tare on the gross account. Your next, in answer to the present, unless you come *propria persona*, will give, I think, a pleasing relation of agreeable interviews with other friends.

"It was a month yesterday when we got safe home, through Divine goodness, from Philadelphia, after a pleasant journey and an absence of twelve weeks wanting a few days. I was present at the audience of the Dutch Ambassador at Congress, but will write you nothing further about it. Saw the Grandees of America, and freely conversed and intermixed with them, and found them to be flesh and bone, and to possess passions and infirmities like myself. Heard enough to convince me more than ever that all bodies of men, Congress not excepted, are best by being looked at from *afar*, and that, if you mean to preserve your rights, you must do your duty and look after them yourself. If they are not worth your care, they are not worth any one's care for you.

"No sooner had I entered within my own State, but taking up a newspaper at Longmeadow upon my return, I learnt, by an extract, said to be taken from the Journals of the House, that our Reps. had beaten the British House of Commons in blundering and trampling upon the Constitution; for that in the case of Williams of Deerfield, who had been returned anew by the town, they had voted in the morning, and that *unanimously*, that he, having been expelled *without a reason assigned*, was eligible by the town ; in the afternoon, — mind, of the same day, — by a great majority, that, having been expelled, he had no right to a seat in the House. He was therefore turned out. *Risum teneatis, amici?* The Gotham managers in this business were the *dux gregis ipse caper* and the first major-general, with whom the plain Parson used to battle it in the Council Chamber.

". . . . We have been looking out for Callahan, who was not arrived yesterday morning. We have had of late good winds ; if he does not get in by Saturday night, I shall fear the worst.

"December 19th. The brig Hope, I judge, is in, having received a letter to-day, but not a word of Callahan ; shall not send my letter off till to-morrow, when in town, with design of putting it into a bag for Liverpool ; till when and thenceforward, I shall remain, as long as I think you entitled to it,

"Your sincere and humble Servant,

"WILLIAM GORDON.

"Dec. 22. Callahan got in at Halifax, dismasted, after a ten-weeks' passage."

From Judge Sergeant.

"BOSTON, December 27, 1783.

"DEAR SIR, — I have just spent a fortnight in Boston, on a special Court, for the trial of certain felonies, — not a very agreeable business.

"I have visited your Fanny, — I know you want to hear of her first ; she grows ; — healthy, at least. I think her countenance better than I ever knew. I made her modesty give me a kiss to carry to Mrs. Sergeant; this, with some chit-chat about her Pa, was our entertainment.

"I expected by this, to be sure, to have received a line from my old friend. I asked Mr. Balch if he had one. 'No.' I asked if he had written to you. 'No, he had rather write to Governors, Judges, Ministers, Critics, &c., than to folks that laid up letters, and could produce them eight or ten years hence against him; he could talk and prate to you, but *litera scripta manet.*' All this does not terrify me. Now for news, if your acquaintance have not been beforehand with me. Peace and plenty seem to have met together and kissed each other; our army is now nearly disbanded, without trouble, tumult, or confusion; our soldiers, in general, return home very far from bad citizens. Trade you left in a tumult, like a pool of water where some solid body had been thrown. The waves have been gradually, one after another, lessening, and will, in the spring, I trust, flow in a regular, smooth channel. My great fear is the scarcity of money, which will unavoidably be great from the continual drains for Europe.

"A Bank is now setting up in Boston, the capital to be $300,000; I imagine it may begin to operate in March next. I trust it will prove of public utility. Dr. Cooper has been dying all day, of a lethargic disorder attended with a fever. We had some alarm lest you were on board Callahan, who has at last arrived at Halifax, but not here yet. I don't know but one poorer man than myself,— that is our treasurer; his creditors are more numerous, and nearer home than mine; this must be my excuse for not remitting to you long before this the money I promised you in August last. I hope soon to be able to do it. Hope is the last thing that forsakes us.

"Next February term our honours are to appear in robes. What a figure we shall make! Must pray you not to neglect sending me the wheat I wrote about; it is said to have come from Farmer Duckett, near London.*

"Pray write to me as soon as possible; to receive a letter from London will exceedingly gratify the pride of

"Your sincere Friend and humble Servant,

"NATH. PEASLEE SERGEANT."

From James Sullivan, Esq.†

"BOSTON, January 8, 1784.

"MY DEAR SIR, — Although I have nothing to write which can in any manner entertain one who now is bathing in Helicon, and breathing in the air of Parnassus, I cannot deny myself the pleasure of writing you a line. You have seen from the very direction of it that it is from the hand of the only one amongst your numerous correspondents who does not know how to write.

"We have got a Magazine on foot. The first number, which is now considered as an abortion, was rascally; the second, which claims the birthright, and is now looked upon as the oldest son, is tolerable; but we want your assistance, and now, while I think of it, the Saturday Paper is out of credit since you left us. I send you two papers to let you know that one of the Muses ventured to stay after you left us. How long she will tarry is very uncertain, and

* I wish I knew whether Farmer Duckett was found by this lucid address.

† Mr. Sullivan at this date was a Commissioner to settle affairs between the States of New York and Massachusetts. Though then only thirty-nine years old, he had already been King's Attorney for the county where he lived, a Member of the Provincial Congress of Massachusetts, a Judge of the Superior Court of Massachusetts, one of three gentlemen sent on a difficult commission to Ticonderoga, a Delegate to the General Congress, and a Member of the Convention for forming the State Constitution, — a remarkable record for so young a man. Later he was Governor of the State.

perhaps you will add that it is no matter, unless she is more propitious than she seems to be in the enclosed production. This you ought to say while you are in your haughty Island, where contempt of America is a cardinal virtue.

"I am planning to get Belknap to settle in Brattle Street Church; how it will be I know not. John Eliot is about being joined in holy matrimony with Joe Treadwell's daughter. Joe is a high Universalist, but John is content he should go to Heaven with as many as he can carry in his own way, provided he can obtain the girl and be in her paradise.

"Our state of Politicks is like that of all the world, — the outs and the ins are at quarrel; trade is dull, I hear, religion is still heavier, and honesty cannot bear our cold seasons. The governor [John Hancock] is sick, and his friend Adams is not very well. The Judges will dress in their robes at the next term; the freedom of the press will be exercised on the occasion.

"The late measures of Britain to stop our trade with her Colonies will throw the States into a ferment, and spirited measures will be taken, which will do much injury to the trade of both nations. Why Great Britain cannot be prudent enough to be our factors, and take all the advantage of our trade, I do not conceive; but folly seems to be their fate. They are buoyed up with an expectation that we shall be driven, by the weakness of our Federal Government, to seek protection from England; but this is all delusion. You may rely upon it that, though our calamities may drive us to accept a monarchy, they will never drive us back to England again.

"I am with great regard, esteem, and friendship,

"Your humble servant,

"James Sullivan."

Extract from a letter from Rev. Jeremiah Belknap to Rev. John Eliot.

"DOVER, N. H., January 26, 1784.

". . . . I have another letter from our friend in England, dated November 12. He mentions having dined in company with Mr. Adams, and breakfasted with him at his lodgings, and says he found Mr. A. very conversable and agreeable and pleasing. Was there any intimacy between them heretofore? If not, it seems there is now, and it may be of an advantage to our friend if this were known in Boston, especially among the higher ones. I do not therefore wish you to observe a Masonic taciturnity on this subject, as I certainly do on another, which is this: he speaks of his just having returned from a thirty-seven days' tour into the country, and after mentioning the importunity of friends, and his not being able to get time to visit them, he concludes his letter thus: 'I have not seen my friend Mrs. Haley these eight weeks. She knows that I am returned from the country, and I must visit her this instant.' Now, my friend, you have the Masonic light, which, without a compliment, I suppose is at least equal to the boasted second sight of the Caledonian Bards. Tell me whether, by the aid of your magic lantern, you can discover any consanguinity between this paragraph and the conclusion of a letter I lately received from Portsmouth. 'Adieu; I must converse with my angel.'*

* The conclusion of a letter from the same Mr. Eliot to whom Mr. Belknap was writing, which is still preserved. Mr. Eliot was then visiting Miss Treadwell, who lived in Portsmouth, and to whom he was soon after married. Mr. B. distributed jokes and badinage rather impartially, it seems.

"We have had it announced in the papers that the above-named lady is about embarking for America, to collect the debts of her late husband. May we not expect our friend in the same ship? But this is a matter of delicacy. He also speaks of dining with the Revolutionary Society, on the 5th November, when this toast was given among others: "May every arbitrary Government experience a Revolution, and every Tyrant meet the fate of Charles the First.' So that you see if a man is to be known by his company, our hero will stand high in the catalogue of Revolutionists.

"Yours,

"Jere. Belknap."

Mr. Eliot returned to Boston in May, 1784, after an absence of eleven months. He did make the voyage with Mrs. Hayley,* but Mr. Belknap's joking suggestions had no foundation. In August 1784 he wrote as follows to Mr. Belknap: —

"I should be very happy to have it in my power to write to my friends as often as they wish me to do; but the increasing calls of my own business, and the attention I am obliged to give to the settlement of Mr. Green's estate, are much more than enough to take up all my time.

*Mrs. Hayley was the sister of the notorious Mr. John Wilkes, and, from all accounts, was as ugly as he was. I believe a stronger measurement could not be given. Mrs. Hayley married, in Boston, a wealthy Mr. Jeffrey, uncle of Mr. Francis Jeffrey, the distinguished Edinburgh lawyer and editor. She lived in a beautiful house on the easterly slope of Pemberton Hill, with fine trees, lovely gardens, and green terraces around it that commanded charming views of town, harbor, and islands. What is the recompense for the loss of that breezy hill and brilliant prospect? Its place is filled by a mass of brick, where lawyers congregate. The only relic of Mrs. Hayley that I know of is a beautiful China dinner set, with her initials on each piece, that has been long in the Prescott family.

In one view I do not regret my perpetual hurry. It takes off my mind from my very painful solitary state. I neither pay nor receive visits; to both of which, separate from business, I have no inclination. I have seen Mr. Howard but one evening since my return, John Eliot as seldom. I am concerned at my solitude, not only on my own account, but on my dear Fanny's. But where can I find a wife and mother? . . . .

"I have purchased my good friend Mr. Amory's house; or rather I have contracted for it, and have the deed, though I have not yet paid for it. I did think to move this fall. I have just determined that I shall not. Why should I, if I have no one to take possession with me? The present abode is good enough for me, though almost filled with goods. Where are your books? I wish they would come from Philadelphia. Let your people send the money for Goldsmith; I want every farthing I can call for.

"Yours in much haste,

"S. ELIOT."

My father had been much troubled, while in England, by hearing of rumors that he wished to marry, and by Mr. Walter Barrell's advice that he should do so. He wrote of this to Mrs. Andrews, with much annoyance and trouble, and came home to great loneliness and sadness, which he forgot only in hard work.

The house he says he had contracted for was a very handsome one for that period, filling, with its out-buildings, the whole space now covered by the Albion, on the corner of Beacon and Tremont Streets, and extending to the stone houses in Beacon Street. It was a wooden building (of three stories and an L behind), fronting on

Tremont Street, with four tall poplar trees before it. A large wood-shed, and capacious stable and coach-house, were on Beacon Street, enclosing a pretty garden and a large paved yard. It was not till July, 1785, that he removed there, probably driven from the Dock Square house by accumulating goods. Fanny, then nine years old, Hannah, and black Peter formed the household. It was time for the change; he was now forty-six years old; business had prospered with him; he had abundant means and a natural taste for social and hospitable action, and another home was necessary for such enjoyment. Miss Hannah described to me something of the change: —

"In the old house, dear, *we* had but little company; in the new house all but everybody, — company forever, — every Englishman that came to town." "Mrs. Hayley?" "O yes, whenever she was in town, there was always a great party for her. *We* had one girl after we went to the new house, but I had all the care. I used to make all the things for company, — jellies, pies, cake, soups, and everything; and there was always sights of things; I don't know how I ever got through it all; 't would kill me now. Mrs. Andrews and Mrs. Job Prince used to receive the ladies, and after dinner they 'd come up the front stairs, and I met 'em on the broad landing, and Mrs. Hayley would give me a dollar and say, 'I know we give you a great deal of trouble.' Then they would go all over the house, — up into the upper story that was n't finished then, — and, O, they did enjoy themselves like queens! Well, dear, I don't know how I should have got through such times if your father had n't been contented; but he was one of them that always knew what he wanted, and when anybody tried to please him, and he always spoke kindly to me."

In spite of such social meetings, those days must have been lonely and full of care. He wanted some one to share his interests and his prosperity, and to guide his young daughter. There was a terrible blank in his life, and none to fill it.

One day in January, 1786, a young lady went to Mr. Eliot's store in Dock Square and made some purchases. She was an entire stranger to him, but while serving her he was so much struck and attracted by her appearance and manner that he determined, if possible, to learn her name and home. She wished to take her purchases herself, but, with resolute adroitness, he prevailed upon her to allow him to send them to her. The address given was "Miss Atkins, at Mrs. Benjamin Lincoln's, Tremont Street, next the Stone Chapel," opposite to which was Mr. Eliot's new house. Mr. Eliot, losing no shade of interest and curiosity, soon obtained an introduction to Mrs. Lincoln and Miss Atkins, through his friend, Mr. Christopher Gore; and his first impressions rapidly strengthened into such vehement feeling, that he determined to win her for his wife, if he could. This was not so easy as he might have wished. I give part of a letter on the subject written to his sister.

"*To Mrs. Ruth Belknap, Dover, New Hampshire.*

"BOSTON, March 11, 1786.

"MY DEAR SISTER, — . . . . I will go on to a much more pleasing subject, and inform you with pleasure, as I know it will give you pleasure, that I have seen and become acquainted with a lady who has engaged my esteem, respect, and love, and in whose heart, if I can make an interest, I shall esteem myself favoured of Heaven. Miss Atkins, of Newbury, is the lady, to whom I should bless God were I to-morrow to be united. She has not any money, but I conceive her worth to be beyond rubies.

"I will give you her character from the closest inquiry of one well qualified from domestick intercourse with this amiable girl, and my own strict observation in two months' acquaintance.

"Know, then, my sister, and, what is more, my friend, that she is a lady of open professed religion and real virtue; of good sense, sentiment, and delicacy; of strong attachment to her relations, not as such, but as those who have in every view approved themselves her friends, and because they have intrinsic, abstract merit. And what, I had nearly said, is more with me than anything else, she is a person of great softness and tenderness of nature, of great candour, sincerity, and truth. Bred up in the school of adversity, and deep read in lessons of distress, she has a tear ever ready to soothe sorrow, and I believe, if Heaven had given the power, her hand would always be open to its relief.

"My connection with this lady has, by much manœuvre on my part, in order to gratify the most timid and diffident of all human beings, — this dear Miss Atkins, — been kept perfectly out of view of the prying eyes and busy tongues of this idly curious town till last week, when it burst at once from its uncommonly fortunate concealment. I should have mentioned a material circumstance in this good lady's description, — she is very fond of children. Fanny dined and spent the afternoon with her at Mrs.

Gore's, say three weeks ago, unknowing even my acquaintance with Miss Atkins. Miss Atkins herself was good enough to tell me that upon the child's instant entry she gave her a look that pierced the inmost recesses of her soul; that before dinner Fanny was rather shy and reserved, but after dinner she grew more free; and having sat some time where she happened to have a seat, she took her stool and carried it to Miss Atkins's side, where she planted it, sat down, put her little hand into Miss Atkins's muff, and attached herself to her for the residue of the afternoon. All this was noticed by Mrs. Gore and minutely related by her also. Fanny came home full of Miss Atkins to me, whom, you may be sure, I did not appear to know much about. The report of last week has met her ear; she has been in rapture at the thought of her being her mamma, as I pray God she may be. I will endeavour to inclose a copy of a letter she has written to this lady, who left this town a week ago for Newbury; every syllable (uncorrected) is her own, whether blameworthy or praiseworthy.

"I have thus given you a very full account of my present situation. May Heaven give me success. Give my best love to Mr. Belknap; tell him I am very sensible that I am much in his debt in writing, but beg his excuse at present. I am much engaged in preparing letters for London. I am also pleasingly obliged to forward letters very frequently to Miss Atkins and her connections, so that my hands are full of a business that I never was and never shall be fond of. Tell Mr. Belknap that Sam [his son] is well, and has been, these three months, every night but one in the week, to the best school I could find.

". . . . I wish most earnestly to be soon at Newbury. I

am miserably detained here at present. I should like a letter from you when at Newbury. Do write me immediately on getting this, under cover to 'Mr. Geo. Searle, Mercht., at Newburyport.'

"I have said I have written several times to Miss Atkins; I have not yet the happiness of any reply. I flatter myself that her dear modesty and diffidence are the only causes of her silence. I hear constantly from her brothers.

"I am, your sincere Friend and Brother,

"S. ELIOT."

As juvenile productions of that period are not common, I give the letter that was enclosed. Miss Fanny was then ten years and two months old.

"*To Miss Atkins, Newbury.*

"BOSTON, March, 1786.

"MADAM, — Ever since the day I had the pleasure of spending with you at Mrs. Gore's, I conceived a peculiar liking to you, which was heightened by your very kind treatment of me. But never did I harbour the pleasing thought that there would be a nearer attachment. Miss Hubbard was the first that I heard it from, and indeed Madam, it gave me singular pleasure, when I had some hope it was true. I asked my Papa about it, and he promised in a week's time he would tell me, but thinking that time too long to be debarred from a thing that would give me such real pleasure were it true, I prevailed upon my Papa to tell me last evening. I have from what he told me some little information, and apply to you, Madam, for further.

"I mentioned you to my Papa, when I came home from Mrs. Gore's, and indeed, there is nobody that I should like so well for a mamma, or that I think would make a better than Miss Atkins.

"I beg you would honour me with an answer, and remain in the due time,

"Your affectionate

"FRANCES ELIOT."

Miss Catherine Atkins* was the daughter of Mr. Dudley Atkins, of Newburyport, "a gentleman of education, intelligence, and good-breeding." His father was a Captain in the British navy, who, coming to reside in New England, brought with him his children (their mother being dead) and a good fortune. About 1728 or 1729, Captain Atkins married the daughter of Governor Joseph Dudley, a widow, with one daughter. I have often heard this lady spoken of as very beautiful and attaching. She married Mr. Chambers Russell. Dudley Atkins was the only child of this marriage.

The Dudley family was held in great distinction in the little town of Newbury, having wealth enough to live handsomely, and being fond of keeping up all the forms and ceremonies of the day. The gold-headed cane, white gloves, and lace ruffles produced their natural effect, while the kindliness and good qualities of the family commanded the affectionate respect of all who knew them.

Why Captain Atkins chose Newbury for his resting-place

* For much of the succeeding sketch of my mother's family, I am indebted to a short manuscript memoir of my grandmother, Madam Atkins, by my cousin, Miss Lucy Searle, who was brought up by her, and who wrote it after the death of Madam Atkins, in the constant companionship of those who knew every fact.

is not recorded. He liked apparently to enjoy his fortune in freedom, brought with him English habits and manners, and continued an Episcopalian. He sent his son Dudley to Harvard College, where he was graduated in 1748, at the age of eighteen. The young man did not connect himself with either of the professions, and only occasionally engaged in business, and in 1752, four years after leaving college, he married Miss Sarah Kent.

Miss Kent's father, Colonel Richard Kent, "was a man of consideration, had a large landed property, and was a Representative in the General Court in Boston." He lived on Kent's Island, about three miles from Newbury, which was entailed upon his oldest son by a first marriage. His other property he left to his daughters, but as it was not sufficient to make them independent, it is said he would have broken the entail, had not Mrs. Kent objected to it. This implies rather an uncommon character in Madam Kent, as she was always called, and tradition confirms the impression. "She was the daughter of Rev. Nathaniel Gookins, minister in Cambridge, and granddaughter of the celebrated Major-General David Gookins, who is spoken of as 'the constant, pious, and persevering companion' of the Rev. John Eliot in his labours for the Indians." Miss Gookins was for some time under the care and instruction of Rev. Mr. Bradstreet, a distinguished clergyman in Charlestown. She first married a Mr. Carter, and had five children. Her second marriage, to Colonel Kent, was a happier connection; they had one son and three daughters, of whom Sarah was the youngest. "Madam Kent possessed a sound understanding and great benevolence, and was a most sincere and pious Christian, with nothing of the austerity and bigotry so common at that period. She used, on winter evenings, to gather her children about her, and read to them such books as Mather's Magnalia, Sir Charles Grandison, or some work on English History. She was thoroughly imbued with the teachings of the best Book, and by these endeavoured to guide and direct her children." It was one of Madam Kent's rules that no stranger should leave her home till his wants were supplied as far as possible, and such hospitality in those days was often important.

Colonel Kent removed from the Island to Newbury, and there, after his death, Madam Kent opened a small shop in her house, and by labor and wise care brought up her children in comfort and respectability. By means of one of her charitable deeds, many particulars of her life, family, and times might have been preserved to us, could we have measured the interest they would now possess. But in youth's vivid interest in the present, we did not estimate the treasures of memory held by the dear old lady we loved so well.

A little girl named Nanny Huse, being sent one day to Madam Kent's shop, she was so much attracted by the child's manners and sweet looks, that she interested herself to find out her family and condition; and learning that she was destitute of friends as well as means, she took her into her family, and there she remained faithful and devoted to her kind friend, till the death, not only of Madam Kent, but of her daughter, Mrs. Burt, who left her an annuity. Years later, when paralysis had partially disabled her, Miss Atkins, a granddaughter of her benefactress, took her to her home, where she died, tenderly cared for, in 1822. "Aunt Nanny," as all called her, formed one of the many charms of that cheerful home in Newbury, —

the gathering-place of children, grandchildren, and hosts of friends, who might have been supposed to be equally related, so many were permitted to call her "Grandmother," and Miss Atkins "Aunt Becky." Aunt Nanny was always on hand, when the young visitors arrived from Boston, with bright, cordial welcome, and eager attention to their comfort and pleasure, moving about in her dark stuff dress and white apron, a square muslin kerchief crossed over her bosom, her gray hair drawn smoothly back under a linen mob-cap, and with such a sweet smile, and gentle, loving look in her brown eyes, that merely to look at her seemed to make us better and happier. The great-grandchildren of her early friend desired nothing better than to be caressed and admired by her, and to listen to her stories of old times.

Miss Sarah Kent, the youngest daughter of Colonel Kent, was noted in her youth for gayety and cheerfulness, — the tokens of a strong and healthy character, that helped to sustain her through a long life of much sorrow and heavy cares. She attracted the love of a circle of young friends by her qualities and mental powers, for neither beauty nor wealth belonged to her. Her features were large but refined; both lips were thin, the upper one long; her chin expressed decision and firmness; her eyes were bright, but a cast in one of them was a serious blemish. Her figure was tall, upright, and slim, her motions were dignified, and it was said she had "a winning, gracious manner," that, combined with her animation, strong, cultivated mind, quick wit, and generous, active sympathy, won devoted friends of all ages, and from the most intelligent circles. In her later years, well-earned self-reliance, costly experience, and strong feeling, led her to a frankness of remark and advice, that sometimes overawed her young friends and disciples; but her tact and ready sympathy soon restored ease and courage, and they gained mental strength from the tonic application.

When she was seventeen, she proved one night the courage and presence of mind that were always afterwards such a support and blessing to those under her care. She had remained reading in the parlor after every one had been long in bed, and when preparing to go herself, in attempting to fasten a back-door, she felt some one pressing against it. Opening it immediately, she found two sailors, who, when she asked their business, pretended they wanted something from the shop. Choosing to appear to believe them, she led them through the house to the shop, gave them what they asked for, and dismissed them by another door. Whatever their intentions had been, they gave her no annoyance beyond the first alarm, which she had so well controlled by her firmness and self-possession. She used to tell her grandchildren that, when she was young, her health was not good enough for sewing and reading, but that she always had enough for walking, running, and dancing! Heavy cares and responsibilities so filled the larger part of a long life, and were so faithfully sustained, that strong foundations must have been laid in those years which she represented as so thoughtless. She taught the many young people under her care and influence, by example as well as precept, never to lose a moment, nor to let any faculty diminish by inaction, and, while stimulating their powers, she had the skill and tact, to make them not only enjoy work, but believe themselves useful.

Within my remembrance, — when time, infirmities, and the devotion of her children had lessened care and anxiety,

— her chief delight was in watching over a large garden, where vegetables, flowers, and fruit flourished under her skilful direction, and where arbors, seats, and a swing, made youth happy, after the allotted time for following her steps with basket, trowel, and other implements had passed. Another charming picture in my memory is that of seeing her spin flax on a small, highly finished English wheel, — her figure perfectly upright, her dress a delicate shade of light-brown stuff, a square kerchief of white gauze, or transparent "mode," crossed in front, with a simple cap (almost like a Quaker's) of the same material, covering her smooth white hair. In the next room, sometimes in the same, the daughter whose heart and life were devoted to sustaining and cheering her mother's hours, standing by the large wheel, almost as tall as herself, drew from it substantial yarn, with that deep resonant *whirr*, of which I can find no illustration, — a sound by itself, — unknown to the present generation.

Miss Sarah Kent, in her youthful castle-building, asserted that she would never marry an only son, a man younger than herself, or one who was not occupied by some regular business; but when she said so, she had not seen the young Dudley Atkins, who, including in himself all these objections, proved his power to overcome them. Their attachment was strong and enduring.

On one point there was a great difference of opinion and feeling between them, and but for the good sense and liberality of Madam Kent, much trouble to the young people might have grown from it. Mrs. Atkins had stipulated before her marriage — from a strong prejudice against the Episcopal Church, to which Mr. Atkins belonged — that she should be permitted to attend the church of her youth,

— the Rev. Dr. Lowell's; but, after a few Sundays of attendance at different churches, Madam Kent entreated her daughter, if she could overcome her repugnance, to leave her and accompany her husband to the Episcopal Church. This she did, and became much attached to the service, and the comfort it gave her was conspicuous. Liberality, however, was not only an inheritance, but a part of her own growth; and her respect and friendship were almost equally given to Bishop Bass of the Episcopal, and Mr. Cary of the Congregational Church (the latter the successor of Dr. Lowell), both of whom were her devoted friends during their lives.

Mr. Atkins, not having been bred to business, was unfortunate in various undertakings, and suffered severely from his disappointments. An only son, unaccustomed to restraint or self-denial, of a generous, genial nature, — the consequences of failure were hard for him to bear. Then it became evident that his wife was gifted with the power to sustain and cheer him. She would assure him that nothing was needed for the family, receive his friends with cordial hospitality, and relinquish luxuries and conveniences for herself. While the family increased, the means of living diminished. Six children were to be provided for, — Mary, Joseph, Hannah,* Catherine, Dudley, and Rebecca.

Of course the Dudley, Kent, and Atkins families were sturdy loyalists, and equally of course, as the spirit of the people rose against the Government, those who adhered to it were objects of suspicion and watchfulness. In 1764, when the revolutionizing Stamp Act was to go into opera-

* On the birth of Hannah, Mrs. Atkins had the courage to discard the habitual swathing and bandaging of young infants, and, though encountering the fears and expostulations of adherents to old customs, her example was soon followed, and babydom was free.

tion, those called Tories were supposed likely to be commissioned to receive and circulate the Stamps, which those who were not Tories were determined should not be distributed. One night a tumultuous mob had gathered in Newbury to overawe and protest at least, and came to Mr. Atkins's house demanding to see him. Three Tory gentlemen were staying in the house while attending the Court in Newburyport, but every one was in bed excepting Mrs. Atkins. She opened the door and stood alone before the excited multitude. She asked what they wanted at that late hour? They called for Mr. Atkins, and said they must see him, for he must tell them if he was in favor of the Stamp Act. She told them that Mr. Atkins was in Boston, and that they must go to him for his opinion on that or any other matter; that it was very late, and she begged they would not disturb her family any longer. "We don't mean to hurt you, ma'am," said a leader. "I have no apprehension that you do," she answered. Just then several gentlemen, who had heard that Mr. Atkins was threatened, came to Mrs. Atkins and offered their aid to protect her; but she promptly declined their kindness, aware that it might easily lead to violence, and, saying that she felt no fear, begged them to go home. The mob, seeing her calmness and courage, felt awkward and ashamed, and began to move off, one fellow having the meanness to hold out his hat. Mrs. Atkins threw a dollar into it, and they disappeared, shouting and calling out that she was "a fine woman," "the right sort," &c. Mrs. Atkins closed her door with a thankful heart that the danger had passed, and that the presence of her inmates had not been discovered; had it been known whom she was sheltering, it would have strongly increased suspicion and indignation.

In 1767 Mr. Atkins died, after only a week's illness, of a malignant fever, at the age of thirty-six, in the prime of life and vigor, leaving his widow overwhelmed by the heavy and sudden blow, deep sorrow, and sharp anxiety for the future.

When able to take counsel, she sent for her half-brother, Mr Carter, and Captain Tracy, also a relative, — both men of large property, to whom she might naturally look for kindness and help. She told them that, it being necessary she should do something for the support of her family, she proposed to open a shop in her own house, as her mother had done; that in starting she should need help, and she begged them to tell her if in their judgment there was any more suitable plan. The gentlemen, probably, did not approve of supplying her with goods, and proposed, as a substitute, that she should give up her house, sell her furniture, and distribute her children among her friends. One can imagine how these cold-hearted suggestions would rouse a grieved and vehement spirit, and quicken the tenderness of a wise and faithful mother. "She knew it ought not to be done," declined decisively, and we hear no more of Mr. Carter or Captain Tracy.

It was not long, however, before real and sympathizing friends came to her aid. At this time Mr. Jonathan Jackson, the head of the family so long known in Boston, was living in Newburyport, as a partner in business with Mr. Bromfield, and both gentlemen were Mrs. Atkins's firm friends. These gentlemen, learning her wish, offered to supply her with goods, to be paid for at her convenience, — a generous offer, which was at once accepted; and though the power to pay in money was long delayed, debts of kindness accumulated on both sides. The shop was soon arranged; Mrs. Atkins spared no labor, strength, or ingenuity to add to her resources; she made candles, soap, and potashes, employing a man to collect materials, and help in the work; and by such efforts, with the most exact economy and self-denial, she succeeded in keeping her children with her, and in preparing them to be useful, respected, valued members of society. Truly may her descendants rise and call her blessed.*

A few years later another heavy sorrow came to her in the death of her daughter Hannah, by a terrible fever, which prostrated all the children. The rest were saved, and her sorrow was softened by gratitude.

In April, 1775, came the rising of the people against the abuse of power, and one day a Mr. Tracy galloped through the streets of Newbury, crying "The British are coming, the British are coming!" Mrs. Atkins was not at home, but her five young people, hearing the cry, thought it time for them to be off; they closed the doors carefully, and walked away with the one idea of escaping from the soldiers. A friend, fortunately meeting the young pilgrims, took them to his house; and there the wondering mother found them, relieved from their fears. At this time of alarm and trouble, Tories from Boston sought safety in Newbury and neighboring towns, and those of the same faith in Newbury, thought it best to retreat still farther. Mrs. Atkins, one of the firmest adherents to the English Government, determined to remove to Amesbury, a small village three miles from her home; and, taking the goods from her small shop and some furniture, established herself in a small cottage with a Quaker family. The rooms were

* There is a striking similarity in the characters, circumstances, and conduct of my two grandmothers. I do not know what became of Captain Atkins's property. His son's family did not inherit it.

very small, but it was necessary for the six added inmates to make them smaller by curtains, in order that the places for sleeping, cooking, and eating might be separated, though by little more than fictitious divisions. Here they lived five years in restriction that amounted to poverty, but I remember hearing my mother and aunts often refer to their happiness in those years. Mutual love, intelligent, active minds, the enjoyment from a really rural life, with visits from kind and faithful friends, gave happiness as well as content.

It is remarkable how much of the intellect, influence, and power we have felt in our society originated in little Newbury. I have mentioned Mr. Jackson, the father of three sons, so distinguished and widely useful in Boston; he himself Treasurer of Massachusetts and of Harvard College, Member of the Provincial Congress, and first Marshal of Massachusetts District. I do not know how long he lived in Newbury, but he was certainly in business there in 1767, and was always a faithful friend to Mrs. Atkins. He at one time placed two of his daughters under her care.

The ancestor of the Lowell family, emigrating from England, settled in Newbury, and there his much-respected descendant, appointed a Judge by Washington in 1789, and in 1801, on the new organization of the Court, made Chief Justice of the First Circuit, lived for some time. His sons and grandsons have generously used large gifts and powers amongst us.

Here came, to study under Judge Lowell, "the young, beautiful, and excellent Christopher Gore," who afterwards filled such a series of high offices, — United States Attorney for Massachusetts, Commissioner with Mr. William Pinkney to settle claims upon England for spoliations, Chargé d'Affaires in London when Mr. Rufus King returned from his embassy, Governor of Massachusetts,* and her Senator in Congress. He was an affectionate and much-loved visitor at Amesbury.

Mr. Gore's intimate friend, Mr. Rufus King, of Scarborough, Maine, distinguished in college for his brilliant powers, afterwards of such eminent benefit to his country, having studied with Judge Parsons in Boston, settled in Newbury as a lawyer in 1780, and he also shared my grandmother's admiration and kindness. It is a striking list, and one can well imagine how such friends were greeted by the exiles at the "lion's mouth," as their retreat was called. Mrs. Atkins's manner of receiving kindnesses was striking, her gratitude was heartfelt, yet natural and frank, with a simple dignity, produced by the conviction that she pleased

* In 1809, when Mr. Gore was Governor of Massachusetts, he made a sort of State progress through Massachusetts, New Hampshire, and Maine, in a showy close carriage, with four horses, with his aides, and an escort of cavalry. It was so unpopular an affair that it probably prevented his re-election. In passing through Newbury he stopped with his brilliant cortége at Madam Atkins's modest home, touching and gratifying her by his respect and affection, and greatly dazzling her grandchildren and neighbors. He was then forty-seven years old, in the fullest vigor of his life and powers; his uncommon gifts of mind, person, and manners, developed and rounded by faithful effort, and every advantage during eight years' diplomatic service in England. Few amongst us have combined so much.

Madam Atkins was then seventy-nine years old, delicate and feeble, but retaining her natural vivacity and quick interest, her erect figure and dignity of bearing. She had heard of the honor intended her, and was seated as usual at a favorite window in her arm-chair, with her feet upon a footstool, when a procession of town dignitaries arrived to notify her of the approach of the Governor, and greatly to the mischievous delight of the young group about her (one of my sisters being of the number) the leader of the party, or head official, carried away by excitement or reverence, knelt before her on her footstool, while he made his announcement and received her thanks.

In a letter from Mr. Gore to one of Madam Atkins's daughters, is this passage (I do not know to what meeting he alludes): — "I have done everything in my power to please your mother and Joe, and I hope I have not failed in every point. The love I entertain for them made me completely happy in their presence. Words could not express my joy at seeing your mother. At once I forgot all my sorrows; and what before was to me a mountain is now but a mole-hill. My disposition is such that at sight of a friend whom I love, my troubles all vanish, and nothing but joy is seated on my countenance."

by accepting, and that, if it were in her power, it would delight her to do as much. But, beyond the grace of acknowledging kindness, she was worthy of such companionship as I have described, through her strength of thought and readiness and vigor of expression. Friends were attracted and attached.

At Amesbury, Mrs. Atkins found unaccustomed leisure, and used it for reading, which she said she had never enjoyed so much. Her favorite books were biographies, sermons, essays, and novels, in which she sought aid in her study of character and human life, — subjects that interested her deeply. She avoided, in reading and conversation, gloomy or despondent thoughts, striving always to keep and to inspire in others a cheerful and hopeful spirit. I give here, for the sake of the domestic facts contained in it, an extract from one of her letters to Mr. George Searle, a cousin of Mr. Gore's, to whom she was much attached, and who, two years afterwards married her oldest daughter.

"April, 1777.

"I have at last taken pen in hand to acknowledge the receipt of two letters from Halifax, with what pleasure I need not tell you. Your good mother is with us still, and has her health as well as is common with her, and seems as contented as can be expected, considering everything. I heard she was uneasy in Boston, and last September I sent and desired, if she could content herself to live as we did, that she would come to Amesbury, and am determined nothing shall be wanting in my power to make her happy. Joe [Mrs. Atkins's son] went last September to Philadelphia, was gone about a month, carried a venture, and it turned out to advantage. Soon after his return, he sailed with Captain Tileston for Bilboa, from whence I expect him soon. Commodore [the youngest son, Dudley] is at school yet. His master [Mr. Moody, of Dummer Academy] is not only his tutor, but his great benefactor. Last fall he made some efforts towards getting an education for him, and made application to some near connection, but was repulsed. He was too tender to say anything to me about it, but I heard of it another way. But he told the lad not to be discouraged, he would give him a year's living, and he did not doubt but he could get him entered then. I have as much business here, I believe, as I should have had at Newbury, and, upon the whole, pass my hours very agreeably. Sam and Kit* were to see us about three weeks ago; I think Kit very promising, and I hear Mr. Lowell is much pleased with him."

In February, 1780, Mrs. Atkins returned to Newbury. Part of the family had gone before her, upon roads covered with three feet of snow, leaving only Mrs. Atkins and her son Dudley to follow the next day, but in the night a rapid thaw came on, making it impossible for her to leave Amesbury. What was to be done? Her presence was indispensable in Newbury. Money would have been of no use in the case. The day passed with all the patience that could be summoned, but it was not possible to wait another. Something must be done; and she finally ac-

* Samuel Gore and his brother Christopher. The son, Dudley, was educated at Harvard, and graduated 1781. He studied law, and was for many years Reporter of the Supreme Court, having previously been Collector at Newburyport. He took the name of Tyng on inheriting an estate in Tyngsborough from a Mrs. Winslow, a descendant of Governor Dudley, who was an ancestor also of my uncle. Mr. Tyng was a gentleman of the highest honor and fidelity, a Christian cheerfulness and equanimity, and a kindness and humor that attracted young and old. He married successively two sisters, daughters of Mr. Stephen Higginson, of Boston, and had a large family.

cepted a quaint conveyance arranged by her son. He fastened an arm-chair securely upon a hand-sled, put a hot foot-stove upon it, wrapped his mother in all the warm things they could command, and, with the help of a boy, drew her on the sled about half-way to her house. There the boy gave out, and Dudley could not, with all his good-will, accomplish the rest alone; so he left his mother at a house near by, went to Newbury and procured two strong men, with whose aid the peculiar journey was easily completed.* Mrs. Atkins's house was in the upper part of the town, then thinly settled,—a small, awkward, primitive, unpainted building, an immense chimney in the centre, the roof sloping from a two-story front to the one low story behind; no fence separated it from the road, but there was a small garden attached to it.

In the winter of 1786 Miss Catherine Atkins visited Mrs. Benjamin Lincoln, in Boston.† This was, undoubtedly, a great event in her life of seclusion at Newbury and Amesbury, varied only by rare excursions to Portsmouth and Salem. She was then twenty-eight years old, very handsome, with a quiet and dignified manner; her features were finely formed and proportioned; — her brow noble,

* As Mrs. Atkins passed the house of her friend Mr. Dalton, several gentlemen of her acquaintance, collected there for a dinner-party, rushed out to greet and congratulate her on her novel equipage, with great animation. I have no doubt she gave them even pay in jokes and cordiality.

† Mr. Lincoln was the son of General Benjamin Lincoln, and married the daughter of Mr. James Otis. They had two sons, Benjamin and James. Benjamin had no children. James, who married Miss Stillman, had two daughters, one of whom, Mrs. Henry D. Rogers, is the only survivor. Mrs. Lincoln (Miss Atkins's friend) survived her husband and subsequently married Rev. Dr. Ware, but lived only a short time after this marriage.

high, and beautifully white; her eyes of a rich hazel, soft and clear; her mouth expressed great refinement and sweetness, mingled with decision, and the lips were always freshly red. I have a miniature* painted about this time, representing her hair — dark, abundant, and curled — with a blue ribbon passed through it, according to the fashion of the time. Her height and figure were good, and in her whole person and every motion there was an expression of modest sweetness and dignity that inspired a respect and affection, which intimate acquaintance only confirmed and increased.

My beautiful, my excellent mother! How can I paint her faithfulness, her attractiveness, her animation and quick perceptions, and her retiring modesty; her tender care of her children, her true sympathy with others, her patience in trials and sorrows? Words cannot do it. We say too little or too much. The life and the form it breathed through were in harmony. She maintained a firm adherence to duty without formality, a simple directness of manner that did not wound, a gentle yielding to the tastes and peculiarities of others; while at times a naturally vehement nature would assert itself. Her cultivated mind, strong sense, and the tact of kind feelings, stimulated and moulded by the sincerest religious belief, exercised a power, and won a degree of respect and affection, quite unmeasured by herself.

I have mentioned the strong impression Mr. Eliot received from his first sight of Miss Atkins. There is no record left of her sensations on that occasion, or of the

* From which the accompanying photograph was taken.

effect of his visits at Mrs. Lincoln's and first attentions to herself. She no doubt heard of his respectability, intelligence, and ripening fortunes; but this last feature in the sketch would, with her, rather check than aid his suit, for her sensitive nature had been nurtured with strong teachings as to independence of externals, and the indispensable dignity of never desiring wealth. The following letter, however, shows that Mr. Eliot was hopeful, and that he thought it his duty to petition first for the mother's consent to his wishes.

From Miss Atkins to her Sister, Mrs. M. R. Searle, Newburyport.

"You know before this time, I dare say, a piece of news which, though I was particularly interested, I did not hear till last night. Mr. Lincoln told me he received it from George [Mr. Searle]. A more perplexing affair I never had concern in before. What will be the result, Heaven only knows. I slept about three hours last night.

"Stranger as I am to the character, and impossible as it now appears to come at the knowledge of the most important part, — the domestic, — I am almost tempted to refuse any further intercourse. For I am not pleased with the suddenness of the matter; 't is not possible he is influenced only by his own observations, unless he is of that rank of men we are used to despise, who are seized by an air or a smart speech. And if a character at second hand is sufficient to make him say what I have had hinted, he cannot, I think, have such an idea of the sacredness and delicacy of [marriage] as I have cultivated in my mind.

"I certainly would not trust the most knowing and judicious friend that ever was to choose for me. I am not either prude or coquette. I am not of an age to be governed by fancy merely, nor am I of that prudent class of persons who can sacrifice all other tastes to be gratified in house and maintenance. I would not trifle with any one; but of all people I shall be least disposed to trifle with myself. Most sincerely do I wish to know what is and ought to be. My situation is not so wretched that I must fly from it without knowing whither I am going, nor is it so completely happy but my imagination can figure a something better. But I would hardly consent to go into Paradise blindfold, much less take the most important step in life without knowing what ground I stand upon. His knowledge of my character must come from Kit [Mr. Gore], and if he is a good client, he [Mr. Gore] may wish him as good a friend as I am capable of making.

"But can he be so totally lost to all virtue as to be thoughtless of my happiness, or willingly sacrifice it to his interests?"

[No conclusion or signature.]

From Mrs. Atkins to her Daughter Catherine.

"Never did a mother feel more for a daughter than I have for the last twenty-four hours. I have so entered into your state of mind that I don't think I should have felt more sympathy had I heard of your being racked with pain. Mr. Lincoln was wanting in the knowledge of our family to treat the matter so abruptly; but you say your mind is more composed, which I am very glad of.

"I don't know that I can say anything upon the subject

that will be new, as you know it has been a very frequent one between us. I hope you will bear it in mind, that views of interest must never sway too much, as wealth can never purchase happiness where there is want of esteem and attachment; but I would at the same time caution you against over-refined notions, — an error which I think you the most liable to.

"Mr. Searle gives me a very good character of the person, and I think you will do nothing rashly. Becky is going into town [Newburyport], to make a visit of a few days, and to-day I intend to devote to solitude and thinking of my Katy. I shall say nothing of your coming home, as I shall leave that to your brother and sisters. Dudley is pretty impatient to see you, and I think I need not tell you how much I long to see you.

"Wednesday Morning."

From Miss Atkins to Mrs. Searle, Newburyport.

"My dear Polly, — Did you recollect my fixed aversion to complimentary speeches, my want of belief of my exciting them justly, and my simplicity in answering them, you would not wonder at my agitation. You may as well compare fire to snow, as the language I have heard lately to *any* I ever heard before on the like subject; and when he has uttered the most vehement things, he assures me he has never used a passionate expression, — "'tis only cool reason'; 'tis true this affords me the pleasure of laughing. I do not wish for obduracy of heart, but for dignity of manner most sincerely do I wish; and I am thinking if I cannot behave in that style here, where of so much seeming consequence, what figure I shall make at home. My honours will all be lost, and I be left to make myself a character.

". . . . The hour I mentioned in my last to George was pleasing to me; and if so, it may be presumed not unpleasing to ———. Did not see him yesterday. He is attending the Supreme Court as Grand Juryman. At seven o'clock in the evening came his man with a billet to Mrs. Lincoln, entreating her 'to let him know of her health, &c., as that was all the satisfaction he could enjoy.'"

[No signature.]

From Mrs. Atkins to her Daughter Catherine.

"My dear,—Remember you are in a state of imperfection. If you meet with a character where, upon examination, you find the virtues outweigh the imperfections, you must value them. . . . . A bystander would judge that you were going to suffer martyrdom, from Becky's and my appearance; but I think it a weakness rather than anything else to be so very uneasy. . . . . You will not fail, I'm sure, of representing the circumstances of the family; let him know all the worst; it perhaps may save me the disagreeable task; and let him come, that I may see him, and perhaps we shall all be merry together: who knows? Tell Mr. and Mrs. Lincoln that I love them very much for their attention to you.

"It may be that the representing the state of our family may alter the plan; and if anything of that kind can, don't fail of letting him know the whole. If this is a repetition, you can excuse it, as you know how much my mind has always been in that way. I think the parties cannot be too careful of never deceiving one another in every respect. I don't think there is much occasion for mentioning it to you, but I hope it won't be taken amiss.

"Your very affectionate mother,

"SARAH ATKINS."

[Indorsed, "February, 1786."]

From Miss Atkins to her Mother.

"Saturday Evening.

"MY DEAR MADAM, — I was interrupted in my last to you, just as I was mentioning Mr. E. He has put an amazing degree of power into my hands; whether I shall use it properly is not yet known. I feel it a painful exercise of all my knowledge, and doubts will always be in my mind as to propriety. . . . .

"Were it any one but myself, there would not be half the doubt; but I have been so little used to think highly of myself, that, — in short, what I hear seems little short of romance to me. If I have the least vanity, sure it will be drawn forth now. I have objected to his particular attention to me by the means of Kit; for *I* have not said anything, and I am obeyed as implicitly as you can conceive. He has great animation, strong feelings, and a great propensity to say civil things; but he has so much address, that even the silence and restraint that is desired of him he can turn to his advantage.

"I have learnt from Kit to-day that his apprentices love him and apply to him as to a father; his man-servant has lived with him five years, his maid-servant some time before his wife's death, and he has no thought of parting with either. These things are in his favour, are they not? But the daughter is still a stranger. Mrs. Lincoln intends to ask to have her come and spend a day with us. It will not be wrong, I hope. To go home without seeing her will be letting forms conquer reason, I think."

"Wednesday Afternoon.

"I was happy beyond my power of expression to see Mr. Searle last evening, and in reading the very affectionate letters from you, Dudley, and Becky. I cannot lament my late uneasiness, for it has discovered, if not created, so much friendship and affection in you towards me, that I shall ever view it as a blessing. . . . . George will be a very great support to me. I love him and feel a confidence in his judgment. Your observations were so good to me, though not new, I have read them twice, and shall read them ten times more.

"As to the circumstances of our family being known, it must be done by some one beside me, or not at all, for I cannot do it at present. George is to pass a part of this evening with him, by his very particular request. Mr. Lincoln exclaims, when I talk, 'Katy is a novelty in the history of woman; uneasy that she is too much respected, and wishing to be made ill of, to lessen the warmth of attachment.' You love me, and I hope will be candid. I am afraid of everything. . . . .

"It shall be my study to keep in the proper line; may I *believe*, if with sincerity (my modesty opposes my adding what I wish I could think), I shall do right?

"Adieu, my dear Madam, and believe me to be, with as much affection as possible, your

"C. A."

From Mr. Searle to Mrs. Mary R. Searle.

"NEWBURYPORT. [No date.]

"DEAR POLLY, — I find I shall not get home this week. I think I never but once was more happily employed, and if I do but relieve Katie's mind in proportion as I burthen my own, my happiness will be heightened.

"I got here in very good season, on Tuesday; drank tea at Lincoln's with Mrs. L. and Katie, and a Miss Philips, which, as you may naturally suppose, was an interruption to our enjoyment. Spent the evening with Lincoln at Harry Hill's Club; on our return, found Mr. Eliot, who had also been in the same suffering condition for some hours, the visitor having just departed before we came in. Eliot's first address was very engaging. Katie and I spent about two hours together after the family were in bed. The next morning I had hardly risen when I received the enclosed. Having before determined to make myself as fully acquainted with the man as possible, I had no inclination to neglect so fair an opportunity. Wednesday evening, of course, was spent at Eliot's, in private, uninterrupted conversation, and, I confess to you, I was charmed with the man's candour, pleased with his good sense, and convinced that his views were not only honourable, but disinterested, and his attachment warm and at the heart. After that, you may suppose, I was not his enemy. The close of this evening was also spent with Katie.

"Yesterday morning I wrote you a line; dined with Eliot, C. Gore, and B. Lincoln, and the afternoon Kit and I traversed every height and walk that the town afforded; and to add to my perambulations, as I returned to Lincoln's before dark, Katie walked to the top of Beacon Hill with me, after which I spent an hour or two at Kit's, and the remainder of the evening very agreeably at Lincoln's, Mr. Eliot in company, and no intruders. The two hours after bedtime were, as usual, devoted to Katie and myself. The good girl, when she went to bed, said she was much relieved, and, for my own part, so pleasing a burthen never before engrossed my attention. It has been so much on my mind during the night that I have slept but little, and rose with the dawn to write this journal to you, which, I dare say, will appear very extraordinary, and convince you that something uncommon has induced it."

[No signature.]

What follows, from Miss Atkins, is on the same sheet as the above.

"Yes, my dear Polly, he has taken the burthen from my mind,—that part at least which could be removed. A great share is still remaining. My head is still full, though less painfully than when I thought alone. George is attentive to all that is to be seen, and is as much interested as I wish him to be, perhaps, but cannot tell.

"I had a good night after saying a few silly things to him, which I have not had before for a long time. Thank Dudley and Becky for their letters. I shall never love them enough for the interest they take in my happiness. I intend to write after the family are in bed this evening, if George and I do not talk too long. Mr. Eliot is now in the other room, waiting for my ladyship, that he may begin to read a play, which, I suspect, will be read well, from a specimen we had the other night. Don't let Dudley think amiss of my remaining here; it would be cruel to Mrs. Lincoln to leave her now. I only thought of going to spend the afternoon out, and her husband, from her appearance of dejection, begged me to stay at home, for that was the cause, he did not doubt. I will think of his delicacy when I find my own fail; it shall support my character. I love him for it.

"Adieu. You must love me, or all India's wealth will not make happy

"Your affectionate

"CATHERINE ATKINS.

"Kiss all the little ones for me. I love them almost too much. Should I ever be a stranger to them, it would hurt me."

It is rare to see the course of such strong feeling so simply developed by the individuals themselves; and it seems to me that if I had read these interesting letters as from strangers, I should have been struck by the expressions of fine character they contain. Dignity, truthfulness, modest self-distrust, yet courage and decision, anxiety for the right, refinement, and warm family affection, are all visible, and form a combination that was shown in Mrs. Eliot's whole life, and will keep these letters always a fresh and living picture. The letter to Mrs. Belknap, which precedes them, was dated March 11, and shows that Miss Atkins had returned home previously. Mr. Eliot never willingly waited for what he desired, if his own efforts, or a stimulus to the activity of others, could gain his point. Great must have been the interest and excitement in the small cottage * in Newbury, while preparations

* This ugly primitive dwelling was still standing in 1820, and I often wondered how the family and household goods could find shelter there. Judge Prescott, father of the his-

were made to send so precious a part of the household to a place so distant as Boston then appeared.

On the 14th of May, 1786, Mr. Eliot returned to Boston with his bride, and I can well understand the delight with which he placed this beautiful and intelligent woman at the head of his pretty establishment, — a home won by his uprightness and industry, and arranged and ornamented by his taste and liberality.

Mrs. Eliot left a home enriched by warm affections, dignified and honored by usefulness, mutual service, and the absence of all external luxuries, and enlivened by intellectual intercourse with cultivated minds. She came to take upon herself new duties, to meet new friends, to enjoy the power of dispensing comfort and cheerfulness to many. Faithfully did she use her gifts and opportunities, but the burdens were not small. The young daughter, eleven years old, had hardly had her fair share of gentle and wise guidance, and her characteristics were anything but neutral, — ruling the servants, and, in a great degree, her Papa. The prompt and cheerful obedience that was part of the Atkins creed was unimagined by her then. The servant who had so long exercised the capacities she herself estimated highly, was more accustomed to being coaxed than directed, and the circle of intimates included some strong ingredients. Some of the brothers of the first Mrs. Eliot were free in manners, language, and opinions, loud-voiced, and jovial; Mrs. Andrews was gentle and refined, but she claimed indulgence and admiration, sympathy in sentimentalism and imaginary ills; Mrs. Hayley, besides being fearfully

torian, told Mr. Ticknor that he was attending Court in Newbury at the time of the wedding; that Mr. Eliot drove in his phaeton, with his bays and black servant, to Mrs. Atkins's house; and that the young men of Newbury and their friends thought it hard that a middle-aged widower should carry off their beautiful young townswoman.

ugly, was coarse and overbearing in her manners; and Mrs. Job Prince soon dropped out of the circle, from the absence of any quality that could sustain her in it. It required courage and tact, sweetness and good judgment, in a young lady of twenty-eight, to harmonize and accommodate such materials, when habits of intimacy had been long established, and the style of manners accepted. But it was accomplished. The Messrs. Barrell lowered their voices and restrained their jokes, and both Mr. and Mrs. Andrews became her attached friends.

At that time — as in many succeeding years — newly married ladies "sat up for company" for several days, and it was said that Mrs. Eliot had numerous and admiring visitors. These visits were not returned in the present brief, cool fashion, by bits of pasteboard, but by liberal tributes of time, — a half-hour in the morning, an hour in the afternoon, or a volunteered tea-drinking, according to the degree of intimacy enjoyed or wished for. It was all rather hard for the simple country lady, whose modesty sometimes amounted to shyness, and her humility to self-distrust. She shrank from numbers and from strangers.*

Mrs. Eliot was industrious from habit and preference, and she found abundant occupation in her new home. Fanny had never been at school, and needed patience and judgment in no common degree. Hannah must be guided and instructed; and visitings and much dreaded dinner-parties, and intercourse with new relatives consumed much

* It was Mr. Eliot's delight to see his wife richly dressed, and he occasionally imported from London articles she thought too fine. I have been told how lovely Mrs. Eliot looked in a "white satin cloak trimmed with red fox fur"; and I remember my own delight in her beauty, when dressed in a short, black velvet pelisse, with a deep lace around it, worn over a white dress. It was a favorite amusement to us children to look at the pretty hats and turbans carefully enclosed in a large box.

time. In the intervals of these duties she found refreshment in her natural love of gardening, and soon filled the little space attached to the house with freshness and beauty. Mr. Eliot, whose previous life had been too full of anxious and active cares to allow him to cultivate a love of flowers, soon shared her interest in them, and took great pride in her success. He built a small greenhouse and sent to England for roots, seeds, and bulbs;* and as time went on, the show of hyacinths, tulips, roses, and greenhouse flowers brought successive groups of visitors, sometimes entire strangers, sometimes friends from the busy regions of Dock Square, often sympathising amateurs and gardeners.

The year following Mrs. Eliot's marriage a heavy grief fell upon her and her family in the death of her elder brother Joseph, then master of a ship, on his return from a long and successful voyage. In a violent storm his vessel was driven upon rocks almost within sight of home; every one on board perished, and the ship was wholly lost. Mr. Joseph Atkins had a strong and upright character, that had sustained him under severe disappointments and hardships, and attached family and friends by his frank, generous, and affectionate nature. His earnest desire to aid his mother and sisters, often disappointed, had been now nearly attained; Mrs. Atkins had just removed to a better house in the hope of receiving him; but at the age of thirty, he was lost, and there being no insurance on his ship, a heavy pecuniary loss was added to the grief

* Many long letters still remain from Mr. Eliot's friend, Mr. Havard of London (for whom his second son was named), giving minute instructions for the cultivation of carnations and other flowers and bulbs which he sent out. Mr. Eliot afterwards bought a piece of land opposite to his house, where the Tremont House now stands, and there, for a year or two, vegetables were cultivated under Mrs. Eliot's directions, partly to interest and amuse her boys, who for one or two seasons kept hens and chickens there.

of their hearts. The following letters are characteristic and touching.

*From Mrs. Atkins to Mrs. Eliot.**

"You love me, my dear daughter, which is a balm to my distressed mind, — distressed, but not cast down. I thank my God, who has wondrously supported me in so trying a scene. I believe the prayers which have been offered to Heaven for me have been heard. — I have been called to receive a visitor. I thank my friends for their attention, but I love retirement better than ever. I feel my mind much disposed to conform to my circumstances. You know I have long since been used to a life of economy, so that it will not be so hard to me as to some others, and Dudley and Becky seem resigned. Time will wear off, in some measure, our distress. We are a very harmonious and, I may say, a very fond family. Never were children more attentive than mine. What gratitude does it call for!

"How shall I express my gratitude to Mr. Eliot? He has my blessing. May God Almighty reward him sevenfold! May you, my dearest of daughters, receive every support under such a trial."

From Mrs. Atkins to Mr. Eliot.

"My dear Sir, — I have too long delayed answering your very friendly and affectionate letter; but so it is — I cannot account for it — that whenever I take a pen in hand to express my mind, my passions are so wrought upon that I find myself quite disarmed of that fortitude which, in general, I have been supported with. I have indeed felt

* There are no dates or signatures to these letters.

a heavy stroke. There were not only the ties of nature, but the friend, the companion, the prop of my declining years, in this dear son. But I will not complain. No; I hope never to renounce the faith I have been so firm in, of a Being that is infinite in wisdom and goodness. It has long since been my petition that I might have that which is best for me, and in general I find my mind much disposed to acquiesce in the Divine will. But there are ties of affection, which the God of nature has implanted in the human breast, and how far these affections are to be indulged, is difficult to know. Mine, since the death of my dear husband, have centred in my too dear children; but I will hope that they will be duly regulated."

One other letter I give, probably written about this year.

From Mrs. Atkins to Mrs. Eliot.

"'Don't be too much struck with the glitter of fortune,' you know, is an old maxim with me. More than what gives us the conveniences of life is but a burthen, except that it puts it in our power to communicate to the necessities and pleasures of others. My wishes are granted in having virtuous children. Riches, you know, I never coveted; but that we might be a family of religion and virtue, has been my very ardent prayer; and to have the affection and attention of these children is such a happiness, that I cannot feel very unhappy, though at times I must feel some anxious moments. It is the lot of humanity. If I see care upon Dudley's brow, or any other trouble attending this same good family that I am so blessed in, I must feel.

"The enclosed present was a very timely supply; it has drawn tears of gratitude from me, and let it draw from you both the tear of pleasure; both are pleasing. But let me have from you both affectionate hearts, which to me is more than any other favour. I am sometimes fearful that Mr. E. will think I do not rate high enough what are called the goods of fortune; but you know there are things that very much outweigh them. Your father had very much the advantage of me with regard to fortune, as well as other things. But I always thought it enough that he had my affection."

There was much happiness as well as discipline in the first years of Mrs. Eliot's married life. Both she and her husband were intelligent, in some degree cultivated, high-principled, energetic, loving action, and desiring sympathy; both were impulsive and full of generous feeling, loving books and intellectual companionship, quick in comprehension and refined in taste. Mrs. Eliot had been brought up under very different influences from those surrounding Mr. Eliot's youth. The affectionate and sensitive portions of her nature had been more developed (subject to the habits of repression belonging to the time), religious teachings had been cherished in her heart, and wrought into her life, while love of nature and of all beauty was active in her and enriching. Warm family affection and constant sympathy had been woven into her existence; and as time went on these gifts and graces woke in Mr. Eliot's nature what had only awaited the finer touch, —what had been kept latent by the pressure of hard work, anxiety, and inevitable business companionship. The presence of young children added its discipline and softening power. In May, 1788, my beautiful and brilliant sister Mary was born, and in little more than twelve years from that time a group of seven healthy children filled the house with life and hope.

Mr. Eliot's hospitable and social tastes were certainly not checked by his added blessings. He particularly enjoyed the gathering of friends at dinner at home and abroad, and always claimed Mrs. Eliot's presence when it was possible.* He sought the society of clergymen; a circle, he thought, was never complete without including at least one of the profession, and on Thursday, when the eleven o'clock lecture at the First Church brought many from the neighboring towns, two or three of them often joined our family dinner. His respect for their profession was so great that he used to say he would "like to have all his sons ministers, and all his daughters ministers' wives." Dr. Foster of Brighton, Dr. Richard Eliot of Watertown, Dr. Gray of Jamaica Plain, Dr. Osgood of Medford, Dr. Porter of Roxbury, were frequently his guests; and Dr. Lathrop and Dr. Eckley, with their white, flowing wigs and three-cornered hats, Dr. Freeman and Dr. John Eliot, all of Boston, were, of course, as often bidden to his table. When these venerable men passed away, their successors were kindly welcomed. Mr Samuel Cary, Mr. Buckminster, M. Samuel Thacher, and Mr. Charles Lowell were frequent and cheering visitors, bringing fresh life and new

* I have heard of her presiding at a dinner with a disfiguring swollen face, and, with the same self-sacrificing sweetness, going to one, with a bandaged hand so painful as almost to produce faintness. In those days it was the custom, when the guests were all gentlemen, to send to the drawing-room before dinner a large India china mug, filled with punch of generous mixture, from which each drank in turn. Another peculiarity of the time was the absence of tumblers; silver mugs and goblets were used for cider and porter, but I think wine-glasses nearly satisfied the whole demand. Three-pronged steel forks were luxurious successors to those of two; finger-bowls and richly colored doylies were in use, but napkins were not known.

thoughts, which, however, sometimes startled the backward-looking mind of age.

At the period I am now speaking of (from 1790) it was Mr. Eliot's habit to give annual dinners, in the best style then possible, first to the Governor and Lieutenant-Governor of the year, with some members of the Council and General Cobb and General Knox of the Revolutionary War; and another to the Judges of the Supreme Court and the prominent lawyers; his own clergymen, and sometimes others of the profession, forming important members of the circle. Great was the preparation to gratify taste and satisfy hunger at these favorite and genial meetings, at which the guests did not exceed fourteen or fifteen in number, and which, beginning at three o'clock, generally extended into the evening. Other entertainments were interspersed, when ladies added to the animation, and when strangers, sometimes from England, were to be entertained.

At this period Mr. Eliot relaxed his attention to business, trusting many details to young men he had brought up. He went regularly to his store both morning and afternoon, but often returned for a visit to the garden, or to make a formal morning call with Mrs. Eliot; and in the summer afternoons took great delight in driving the fat bays in the high English phaeton, with Mrs. Eliot and one little child for his companions. When visits were in the programme, black Dalton was perched upon the small seat in front, held the reins, and was ready to attach the portable delicate leather steps, which it demanded no little skill to mount and descend with grace. It was much the fashion in those days to make afternoon visits at the country houses of friends, to take tea and fruit. Mr. Gore's beautiful establishment at Waltham, Mr. Barrell's at Charlestown,

Governor Brooks's modest home in Medford, and Dr. Osgood's, were often the objects of a drive; and on the other side of the town, at Jamaica Plain, Mr. Prince, Mr. Coffin Jones, Mr. Bussey, and Dr. Gray were visited.

Those were animated days, bringing in their train the multiplied cares of young children, housekeeping, and gardening; for the garden and greenhouse had become institutions, exciting family interest and needing constant oversight. Often, during the hours passed there, tributes arrived from the store, — rare fruit, or pigeons bred in the attic, — with little notes, some of them rhymed, like the following: —

"Katy, I send you this to tell
That I am better, though not well,
And having little else to do,
Have set me down to write to you.
But yet a shop 's no place to write,
For should a payment heave in sight,
The Muse's service I must quit,
Nor lose the cash to show my wit.
My wit! which better had been shown
If I had left my pen alone;
But when the itch of scribbling comes,
It is not trumpets, guns, nor drums
Can make us change our rhymes for prose;
For prose is vulgar, rhyme divine,
As I am proving every line."

With this are other rhymes which I like, simply as being my father's, and therefore place them here.

The first portion of the following, I imagine, may be my mother's, as it is marked "C. A., 1784"; the second part is marked "S. E., 1786."

"Whate'er of ill I 'm destined to endure,
Whate'er of passing pleasure to secure,

All perfect Wisdom knows what share of pain,
All perfect Goodness does the whole ordain.
May I ne'er suffer murmuring thoughts to rise,
And, though oppressed, may mercy fill my eyes;
May grateful thoughts, still glowing in my heart,
A powerful aid to charity impart;
That noble virtue may I ever know,
That bond of social happiness below.

"What blest effusion of a female mind,
By virtue tutored, and by Heaven refined!
Indulge thy genius, and improve the age,
And add thy pure thoughts to the moral page;
Then shall the world in Katy's praises join,
While my heart glows with rapture that she 's mine."

"*To my Wife.*

"Katy, I 've often heard you tell
Of the blue violet's fragrant smell;
I 've tried it oft, but still complain,
My frequent trials are in vain.

"Placed in your bosom for an hour,
I hail its aromatick powers;
Whence I conclude the sweets it drew
Were not from nature, but from you."

"*Thoughts in Sickness.*

"My God! should illness cloud my days
Shall it suspend my songs of praise?
Sickness, that, rightly understood,
May give the best, eternal good.

"Sickness may wisdom's truths dispense
And draw to God from flesh and sense;
Danger attends that wretched lot,
In which a future state's forgot.

"I envy not their boasted state, —
The gay, the prosperous, and the great, —
Those heedless beings who employ
Their every thought in present joy.

"The powers of man were never given
To shut out every thought of Heaven;
Another world awaits us still,
And judgment follows good or ill.'

"If vicious here, our fate we know
Comprises every dreaded woe;
If virtuous, every bliss ensues,
Supremely blest who virtue choose.

"Come, then, the most distressing ills,
Come whatsoe'er my Father wills,
Come every grief, in ev'ry form,
If virtue firmly meets the storm!"

In 1798 Mr. Eliot was chosen President of the Massachusetts Bank, the first and then, I believe, the only institution of the kind in New England. It was an honorable trust, and he held it till 1804. Dr. Ephraim Eliot says: "That station was then considered as the highest pinnacle of honour to which a merchant could attain. How different now!"

At this period of the world of little Boston, there were few societies or clubs. Even a volunteer fire company created a strong interest. It was formed of gentlemen who agreed to help to extinguish all fires, and to keep ready for use a certain number of painted leather buckets, canvas bags, and bed-keys for taking wooden bedsteads apart. Every month a solemn committee visited each member's house to examine these important implements, exciting much awe in young minds. A hot supper rewarded their labors, which Mr. Eliot gave in his turn, and occasionally attended those given by his friends. The Church Committee of which he was a member for a time had the same cheerful recompense of a hot supper every month, and no doubt there were other such gatherings of which there are no records. In the Society for the Aid of Widows of Congregational Clergymen — founded, I presume, at a much later date — he took an active and animated interest, and was always ready to give time, money, and labor, though it was under the control of gentlemen of a very different religious creed from his own. The great need of those deserving women would have overcome sectarianism in him, if it had existed. The annual Convention of Clergymen, often the occasion of vehement discussions of creeds and doctrines, was an important day in the family, — so deep was Mr. Eliot's interest, so many queer, country clergymen dined with him, and the debates and personal encounters were so long subjects of narration and of discussion. I do not know whether he belonged to other charitable societies, but have no doubt he gave suitable contributions for their objects. He was liberal and generous, but an exaggerated fear of being thought wealthy and ostentatious made him sometimes refuse, almost sternly, applications made when other persons were present, which he afterwards privately supplied. He particularly disliked subscriptions, and rarely put his name to one. Dr. Ephraim Eliot gives a few anecdotes relating to these matters.

"Mr. Eliot did not wish to be called a generous man; though he gave away annually to a considerable amount, he was always secret about it. He hated subscriptions. An instance: One of his first apprentices, Elisha Sigourney, was in a small way of business; his store was entered at night, and he robbed of three hundred dollars, which embarrassed him greatly. When it was probable that it would never be recovered, Dr. John Eliot (Mr. Sigourney's minister) received a letter, in which was enclosed three hundred dollars, with a request that it should be conveyed to Mr. Sigourney, and not to insinuate or hint from whence it came, if he suspected. It was privately sent to Mr. S., who afterwards told Dr. Eliot (confidentially), that having known of such charities before, he knew from whence it came. Some years after, Dr. E. ascertained that it came from Mr. Eliot. I have been a medium of conveyance myself. On one occasion he gave me a sealed paper directed to the 'Widow McKean,' to be put into the contribution-box at the meeting of the convention of Congregational ministers. But there happened to be two 'Widows McKean,' and when the contribution was assorted, the friends of each claimed it, with not a little pertinacity on both sides, and it was finally proposed to divide it. But on inquiry the sealed paper was traced to me. It was then suspected from whom the donation came. Dr. Lowell ascertained that the fifty dollars was intended for the widow of Professor Joseph McKean, of Cambridge [previously clergyman at the First Church, Boston], and the whole amount was given to her. The other was the widow of President Joseph McKean, of Bowdoin College, who lost nothing by being confounded with the Cambridge lady."

"My instructor, Dr. Isaac Rand, and his father were both rich men; they used to say they had never known a man to raise a fortune by honest methods, — that fraud was always at the bottom. Since the death of Mr. Eliot, I have endeavored to search his character to the bottom. He has been called 'a proud man'; so he was, and so are most people that have become rich; — 'a mean man'; sometimes he may have appeared so, as he always made as good bargains as he could with those with whom he had dealings. They may have thought he was too close with them, but I have never known a fraudulent transaction to be charged to him in my life, nor that he ever kept a man out of his money when it ought to have been paid. In short, in viewing his character throughout, I think it has been as uniformly correct as that of any person I have ever known. Imperfections I have observed, it is true, but they were imperfections only."

This is honest and strong testimony, for relatives stood very near each other in those days, and society was so small, and business operations were so compact, that action and character were generally and to one's family minutely known. Mr. Eliot was much attached to his cousins John and Ephraim, and trusted them confidentially in more matters than his charities. The phrase that no "fraudulent transaction" had been "charged to him" sounds oddly cool from so intimate a relative; for, according to my estimate of his uprightness and impetuosity, any one who had suggested such a "transaction" for his acceptance would not have left his presence by any common or slow process; and, had he known of such faint praise from a friend, his mode of answer would have been marked.

Another of Mr. Eliot's private charities is told by one of his nieces. "There are other instances of your father's charities that might be mentioned. His liberating all the prisoners in the Leverett Street Jail that were confined for debt, by paying the sums due from them, was one I always admired. It was as he supposed kept an entire secret at the time, Mr. Lowell only knowing from whom the money came. Your mother was led by your father's silence on the subject, when so many others were talking of it and wondering from whence the good deed came, to suspect it was from him, and after his death Mr. Lowell told her that it was so."

My last date was 1798; twelve years had passed since Mrs. Eliot's marriage, — years full of active industry, strong influences, and much development; brightened by prosperity, by intelligent and healthy children, and by cordial and loving friends. Care and trouble were, of course, mingled in their lives. Mr. Eliot's health was so nearly perfect that a common cold or any slight illness was apt to occupy his attention and cause depression, though he bore the annoyance patiently. Mrs. Eliot had several severe illnesses; and the bringing up of seven children, with the economy which was the general rule in those days, was a serious matter. There is no need of enumerating the features of such a life; all know them.

The great test of character is prosperity; if that elevates and enlarges instead of contracting the heart, then sorrow and care will add nourishment and strength. I think it was so with both Mr. and Mrs. Eliot. Through many years of radiant prosperity, Mr. Eliot preserved the clear, calm judgment, the exact uprightness and unsullied honor, that had grown from his youth up; a faithful, unflagging attention to what he esteemed a duty, whether great or small, whether demanding personal sacrifice or resistance to persuasion; uniform industry, a constant desire for improvement, a reverent and firm religious faith, watchful care of his children and of all whom he employed, a liberal but modest use of money, and a dignified disapprobation of personal luxury and show.

His temperament was vehement, earnest, excitable; his feelings were sometimes uncontrolled, but the reins were soon recovered. From the brightest light we have the strongest shadow. Excess of virtue even is dangerous, and so is the intensity of energy and self-reliance which is necessary to carry one through sacrifice, anxiety, and hard work. The object gained, the qualities which produced success in action cannot be suddenly pruned down to fit a life of ease. His love of reading rather increased with leisure, though it had always been so strong, and it was fed by boxes of books, ordered annually from the Messrs. Longmans. He had a great value and feeling for books themselves; to drop a nicely bound one troubled him almost as if it had sensation; to skim through a new volume, while cutting it, seemed to him a disrespect to the author, besides being a bad habit for the reader; and to borrow a book was so displeasing, as nearly amounted to a prohibition. There were not many temptations to borrow books in those days. Few were printed here, those privately imported were as few, I imagine, and prices at the bookstores made what was bought too precious to lend.

His children were a great delight to Mr. Eliot. Dr. Ephraim speaks of this more than once. He frolicked and played with them, allowed freedoms and sauciness from the boldest and gayest, that made the shy ones anxious.* An expression of intelligent attention, a proof of knowledge, or a repartee brightened his eye, and gave him a pleasure that he could not wholly conceal, while the personal beauty of some among them was a source of no small enjoyment to him. Yet such was his fear of exciting vanity and self-esteem in them, and so strong was his sense of responsibility, that pleasure and approbation were rarely expressed. Of course this reticence made praise more valued when it came, and the young observers were generally aware when he was pleased or the reverse, without words. We do not always measure justly the quick perception of our tastes and peculiarities by the young minds about us, nor their strong feeling of even unexpressed approbation or disapprobation.

Having suffered so much from all sorts of restrictions in childhood and youth, Mr. Eliot must have felt a deep satisfaction, that, through his industry and success, his children need not have any such experience; yet he thought the dangers of extravagance and idleness so imminent, where necessity did not tyrannize, that he threw over them a little of the shadow of his own early troubles. It was simply a too stern self-control, as every one realized who knew his sensibility and impulsiveness, his liberality, and his almost tearful sympathy with anything pathetic or noble.

Mr. Eliot's ideas upon education were distinct and firm, — more strict than Mrs. Eliot wished, but, with such modifications as she procured, would be constant blessings in most households. As I grow older I perceive that the

* My delightful brother William, the leader in all family fun and frolic, a beautiful singer, and his father's hope and delight, was the most daring in his demands as a child, making his father carry him on his shoulders, driving him by his coat-tails, and exercising other playful tyrannies.

leading principles he wished acted upon had wisdom, foresight, and refinement for their foundations. Unquestioning, instant obedience and silent submission were necessities. Truth was claimed, as open and pure as light; the slightest deviation from it, even under palliating circumstances, was punished. Girls should not go to school to acquire vulgar tricks and companions, and little else; mothers could teach enough to make useful women and agreeable companions, if the children were intelligent; if they were not, home, of course, was their best place. Boys must rough it at school, and learn to fit themselves for life by resisting evil example. Great care should be taken as to reading. Neatness and industry, promptness to serve others, and cheerful amiability were expected, and their absence noted. Mr. Eliot could not bear any carelessness in dress or hair, particularly on the first appearance in the morning; he always remarked if any one sat unoccupied or lounging; he did not like to have ladies, young or old, occupy themselves in their chambers; after the first morning hours the parlor was their place, and their appearance and occupations should be adapted to it; bundles and baskets should not appear in the drawing-room; little children should not talk before their parents, particularly at meals, unless addressed, and the answers must be gentle and respectful. It was forbidden to sit or stand at the window, and if youthful curiosity was too strong, the forgetful one was soon reminded of the law. Young ladies should not go to public places, rarely to parties, they should not walk in the streets merely for exercise,* and, when necessarily out, should not allow gentlemen to attend them.

* Exercise and air were not thought so indispensable as at present; but Mr. Eliot now and then took his children for a sedate walk in the mall, and in winter would take as many as the chariot could hold, to walk on South Boston bridge, then a very quiet and solitary avenue.

It was strictly required that all should be punctual at morning prayers at eight o'clock; that all who were old enough should go to church twice on Sunday, learn and repeat a part of the catechism and a certain amount of hymns, and listen to an additional sermon,* read by Mr. Eliot after the afternoon service. He did not spare himself. In most of these rules and opinions Mrs. Eliot coincided entirely, but her sympathy and tenderness measured better the difficulty that vehement and restless childhood and youth find in submitting to fixed and rather strong laws. She now and then contrived modifications, and procured small indulgences, without, in the least, relaxing authority.

In the matter of instruction, she persuaded Mr. Eliot that his daughters ought to know more than she could teach; and, in consequence, two of them were sent for some seasons to a school kept by a Mr. Cummings, the best that had then been known in Boston; they had lessons in writing from a Mr. Webb, and a little instruction in drawing from an Englishman, a Mr. Smith, a very good teacher. The boys attended, in succession, the public Latin School under Mr. William Biglow.

Of Mr. Eliot's religious opinions, I can only say, they were reverent and sincere, simple and liberal. The strong influence of such men as Dr. Andrew Eliot and Dr. Simeon Howard, both of whom he truly revered, was exerted to form a devout and upright life, candor, and charity. They

* The Sunday was generally a strain upon self-command; the third sermon was a little hard upon the patience of the young ones, but the garden and nursery were safety-valves, and the closing of the reading was a sort of jubilee, for then the mother gathered the little ones about her, and fed them with some dainty, fresh fruit in summer, delicious preserves in winter, — "the biscuit or confectionery plum," — and frolic and laughter were not only permitted, but encouraged.

rejected the stern Calvinism of their predecessors, and Mr. Eliot's whole nature revolted from that system, and from everything that looked like spiritual intolerance or domination. He followed the religious controversies that so stirred the hearts of the people, when strife for political freedom was partially allayed, with a deep and not a silent interest; indeed, in later days, when Dr. Jedediah Morse appeared to desire to extinguish poor little Miss Hannah Adams, he expressed his indignation with such force that to young imaginations Dr. Morse seemed dreadful as Apollyon. Mr. Eliot was a regular attendant at church twice a day, and through all seasons and whatever the weather, even in the worst, always walked. He never sat during the service, and during the sermon leaned over the door of the pew in undivided attention, a slight motion of his head now and then expressing approval; while it must be confessed that the same frankness led him to stand with his back to the pulpit, when the teachings were not so much to his mind. As this occurred only when strangers preached, we trusted they did not recognize the contrast. When the stranger pleased and satisfied, he was generally invited to dinner.

He did not approve of evening lectures, and often rallied Mrs. Eliot upon her enjoyment of the Thursday morning lecture, maintaining that ladies ought to have too much to do at home at that time of day, to be able to indulge in such a pleasure.

Mr. Eliot rarely talked of religion, but when called upon to give up hopes and desires which were like a portion of his existence, his submission, even through great agony, proved the strength of his religious faith.

Dr. Belknap's sudden death, in 1798, was a great shock and sorrow to Mr. and Mrs. Eliot. In the ten years of his residence in Boston, Mrs. Eliot had become much attached to him; his cheerful, amiable temper and active, cultivated mind made him an attractive companion and valuable friend, and she, after his death, proved a most faithful and soothing sister to his suffering widow.

In those days, when fortunes were moderate, and each household was occupied with daily cares and real work, leisure did not promote frequent meetings or many intimacies. Dr. Ephraim says: "Mr. Eliot did not approve of indiscriminate visiting; people were not to happen in; when he desired friends about him he would invite them; and this continued his preference till his last years, when loss of sight so oppressed him that a volunteer call was a refreshment to him." He had no taste for long visits from friends, yet he welcomed Mrs. Eliot's relatives from Newbury with cordial hospitality every season, and proved, by receiving kindly some who had no family claim, that he knew how to make exceptions to his general rule.

Annual visits to Newbury were a refreshment and delight to the mother, and to those of the children who were permitted to go with her. The journey, almost always made with the pet bay horses, was a serious affair of two days, Topsfield being the dreary resting-place for the night. But discomfort only added to the zest of the excursion, and the charms of the home in Newbury would have been potent against a much harder test. We were going to a devoted fairy grandmother, who would give freedom, health, sympathy, and approbation. The feeble were sent to her for strength, the naughty for reformation; and so charming were her modes of restoration from even moral diseases, that one young offender, knowing that the last resort in her case was her being sent to her grandmother, inwardly resolved to postpone all signs of reformation till she was with her. While working in the broad garden, under a kind and sympathizing eye, health and goodness were breathed in together. We were never praised by words, but we felt the pleasure we gave by successful efforts, or even by the mere effort. It was a tonic, happy life, and we came back to quiet home duties, with new powers and resolves. I give a letter written during one of these happy visits: —

"*To Miss Mary H. Eliot* (*from her Father*).

"BOSTON, September 3, 1800.

"DEAR MARY, — I received with much satisfaction your clever little letter by post, and was much pleased to hear your grandmother was well, and should have been glad to have had the same good account of your aunt Becky, whose situation gives me real concern.

"You found less difficulty, I dare say, in writing your letter than you expected you should when I enjoined writing upon you. Thus you will find it through life; when we look at a duty to be performed at some future time, especially if it is one which we have not practised, we are apt to magnify the burden and lessen our capacity of performance; but remember, my dear child, that a strong respect for duty, with a resolute and tolerably well-informed mind, will find difficulties vanish before them, and what appeared in contemplation almost impossible to be effected will be comparatively easy in execution. Patience, fortitude, and perseverance will carry us through any opposition in the path of virtue. A willing mind, that sets itself in earnest to do its best, will soon observe every impediment lessening, and what at first might be perhaps disagreeable will, in a short time, be greatly pleasing. A resolution to do our duty is nearly half the performance of it.

"It seems you are anxious about my hair. I am much obliged indeed by your attention; but do not flatter yourself, little madam, that you have left no one here that can give it a decent appearance. What think you of Fanny? and what do you say of your mother? I will say nothing of their merits on this *head*, but leave it to your own determination.

"I am rejoiced to find you are determined to be useful, for it is as wise and virtuous a resolution as you could any way form. Be assured that a healthy, strong, idle girl is a nuisance in society, and the contempt of all good people.

"Charles, William, and Sam are good boys, behaving very well, and desire their love to you and Eliza. By the by, Miss Harrison, where were your recollections when you wrote, that you omitted all notice of Eliza? I hope your memory will serve you better when you write me next. Give my regards to her, your grandmother, and Aunt Becky.

"Be a good girl, if you value my good opinion and affection, for I cannot — nay, I ought not — to love bad girls, such as you will never prove, I trust.

"Your affectionate Father,

"S. Eliot.

"Little Cate is well, and desires her love to you both, to her grandmother, Aunt Becky, cousins, &c., &c. Tell your aunt Searle that we have some woollen goods just arrived, if she wants any [for her shop]. I have sent a box of peaches to your grandmother, which, I hope, will come in good order, and be pleasing to her. Fanny is at Mr. Barrell's."

I have as yet said little of the oldest daughter of the house, Fanny, who, born in 1776, was, at the date of this letter, twenty-four years old. Her nature and character were so marked, and so different from Mrs. Eliot's habits of mind and judgment, that she was never a neutral element. She could be a pleasure, she was oftener a perplexity. While her own mother lived, Fanny's health and pleasure were objects to which most other things yielded, — a system which produced its natural results, aggravated in this case by a peculiar delicacy of organization, and the mingling of caprice, quick wit, and sharp observation. Seven years of these influences left their permanent effect; during the three next she was almost wholly under the care of servants, and, when Mrs. Eliot took charge of her, little Fanny knew better how to rule others than to govern herself, and knew very little else. She was small, pretty, and active, — a something between a Fenella and an Undine; she disliked occupation, soon wearied of play, enjoyed mischief. What should be the wisest treatment for a child of such peculiarities, must have been an anxious study for the new mamma. For many years she made the most faithful and the most various efforts to attract Fanny's affection, to conquer her restlessness, and to cultivate habits of industry and self-control. Some progress was made, for Fanny had feeling and talent; but taste and capacity were developed in different directions from those approved by the Atkins school. A little playing on a primitive piano, a little singing, a faculty for fancy work and for dress, with ability for more useful occupation, exhibited under special stimulus, finally produced a young lady rather fascinating when in good spirits, but not a very useful or reliable member of a family.

Fanny visited the kind grandmother occasionally, and all other good influences were sought for her improvement and happiness; and, in 1789, when she was thirteen, she was put under the care of Mrs. Higginson and her daughter Hetty, living in Salem. They were true gentlewomen, with much of the stately courtesy and manner of the period, and believing in their inheritance of worth and dignity from their ancestor, the venerated Mr. John Higginson. To enlarge a very limited income they taught young children, and Miss Higginson lived long enough to educate successive generations in Salem, and to receive from each constant expressions of grateful respect. They were truly faithful in their care of Fanny, and were valued and held in true respect by Mr. and Mrs. Eliot.

The letters from Mrs. Eliot to Fanny, written at this time, are so expressive of both characters, that I give a few of them: —

"*To Miss Frances Eliot.*

"NEWBURY, June 28, 1789.

"DEAR FANNY, — You will be pleased to receive this, as it will inform you that your papa is so good as to consent to your tarrying till Mr. Searle comes for your aunt Becky [Miss Atkins]. . . . . You desire me to write a few lines, just to tell you how everybody does; but it appears to me that alone would make more than a few. However, we are all, in the family and at your aunt Andrews, much as you left us. . . . .

"Now for a few inquiries, which I wish you to make into your conduct. Do you rise early? Do you go to bed early, and without waiting to be bid? Do you try to be useful without being troublesome? Do you avoid asking questions, and all sorts of impertinence? Do you keep your chamber and trunk in good order, or is your slip on one chair, your cloak on another, and the table covered with combs and papers? Do you keep to a simple diet, or has your appetite betrayed you? These are matters you must take care of yourself, as I am not by you, and it is asking too much attention of the friends you are with to do it for you; therefore, 'tis you alone that will be to blame, and you will be the sufferer, if any bad habits are contracted. I shall not be able to procure another visit for you, if this does not do you good rather than harm. . . . .

"Your papa was pleased with your writing; let this encourage you to try more and more to excel. I can write no more than just desire my duty to my mother, and my love to my sister, and remain,

"Your affectionate Mother,

"C. Eliot."

"*To the Same.*

"Boston, July 12, 1789.

"I am very glad that your visit has been not only agreeable, but long enough, and that you are wishing to come home. It would have been, I think, a little strange, had three weeks passed and no desire of seeing home arisen in the time. . . . .

"When the cloth was taken from the table to-day your little sister [Mary, a little more than a year old] took her seat upon it, and as we talked of your coming home, she looked very earnestly at the door, to see you as you entered, full of expectation. She will be pleased at your return, I dare say.

"*To Miss Fanny Eliot.*

"SALEM. [No date.]

"MY DEAR FANNY, — I have taken the earliest opportunity I could find to write to you. We are all well. . . . .

"I hope soon to send you some work; for your time must be a burden, I fear, or at least you wish in earnest, I hope, to employ yourself. . . . . I have sent some cotton with the needles, for you to learn to knit with.

"I do very much rejoice in your situation, I think it highly calculated to improve you. You must write me the course of your employments, your method of learning, and all the little matters that turn up in your way, that I may be able to form a more complete judgment of your feelings and improvements. I shall write you as often as I can. The greatest inducement I can have for frequent writing is your present and future happiness, which I have much at heart. Your letters will tell me all you wish me to know, and I hope that you will be so careful of your dispositions and manners that no one will have it in their power to tell me anything that you will wish concealed. . . . .

"I am too much engaged to write more now, therefore must conclude with repeating what you know I am exceedingly anxious about. Pray be *careful; think*, that you may *act* well, — that you may make your friends happy, and believe me, not one of all the number will rejoice in your welfare more than

"Your affectionate Mother,

"C. Eliot."

"Boston, December 30, 1789.

"My dear Fanny, — To those who seek most the improvement of the heart, such seasons as the present are generally used in serious recollections of the various occurrences of the past year, that no mercy or correction may pass unnoticed, but each, with due reflection, be marked for future government. May you, my dear, collect your best abilities, and, with careful industry and firmness, pursue some line of thought that will lead you to a knowledge of yourself, your true character. Let not the partiality of friends, or the more influential flatteries of self-love, disguise from strict examination those whisperings of your mind which are the admonitions of your Heavenly Father. Think for one moment on this single idea, and it will give such motives for attention to the still voice of conscience, as can hardly be resisted by a mind unadulterated by vice.

"To a mind of genuine sensibility the entrance upon a new year gives rise to many ardent wishes. Hopes of future good will employ many of the retired moments of the young and happy. Let yours be used to fix in the best manner you are able firm resolutions to *be good*. For this purpose, if you recollect and attend to those things you have heard and read, which you feel have had the best influence upon your thoughts and conduct, they may serve you again. Many more are still in reserve for you. Bend your wishes with ardour to grow in virtue, and you will find assistance ever ready. I think to keep a small memorandum-book in your pocket, in which you may write any short sentence that strikes your mind as useful, will help you. . . . . As you have no book that I think so convenient as mine for this purpose, I will lend it to you till its place can be supplied with one of your own.

"As a proof of my hopes that your new resolutions will be firm on the side of virtue, I send you the needle-book you have been so solicitous to deserve. May it prove a stimulus to something worthy each time you see it. . . . .

"You will not fail to let me know when your pocket-money and work are nearly out, as I shall be ready to supply you with both. . . . .

"You will be pleased to hear that Mary is so very fondly attached to you that if she hears your name, or thinks of you without, it is with difficulty we pacify her, she is so very anxious to have you appear at the moment. . . . . The hair in the book you will know to be hers, and that I should not have sent it, but that you have so often desired it. Adieu; be good, that you may be happy, and lovely to all, but particularly to

"Your affectionate Mother,

"C. Eliot."

"February 14, 1790.

"My dear Fanny, — . . . . The little book you enclosed for your papa's inspection I saw, and was pleased with the method of arrangement and the economy; but why, in all the time you have been absent, you have never met with one person to whom you wished to give sixpence or more,

I cannot conceive, or, if you have, why you have denied yourself the pleasure. Surely, you could not so far mistake my advice as to think I meant, by economy, to debar you the satisfaction of giving a part of the little you have to a deserving person you might help or please. It was not in all my thoughts, and I am sure your father will be happy to supply you with money for such purposes."

"February 27, 1790.

". . . . Be careful to observe what you read, and when you want employment make such little extracts as strike your mind as useful. This method may store your mind with good sentiments. But the best and most useful knowledge is gained by observations upon real life; the sight of one object of distress will have more lasting effect upon a feeling mind than reading many imaginary descriptions of the deepest sorrow. . . . . Your heart, my child, is the object of my most solicitous attention. 'T is there you must fix your foundations for present as well as future happiness. If that is good and rightly tempered, you will be safe, and your friends will all be happy in you.

"Have you repeated lately the fine poetry you learnt from the Lyric Poems?

"Shall I tell you that I was as much, if not more, pleased with the present you sent Mary last, than with any piece of work I have ever seen of yours? It is a proof of attention, neatness, and industry, three very important articles in the list of good qualities, of which you will make yourself mistress if you are what I wish you. . . . ."

I will not multiply even such attractive proofs of strong sense and faithful care of a step-daughter. In 1792 Fanny was again at home, a bright, animated girl of sixteen, quite accessible to the flatteries of her own mother's relatives. She respected my mother, she loved the children while they were pretty and not troublesome, was at times ready to make much effort for them, but often preferred their absence. When happy, she was very amusing. She had talent, but no steady application. As years passed on, she went into a good deal of company, had her intimate friendships and flirtations, passed a day frequently with her aunt and cousins, the two Mrs. Joys, walked and drove with the young Messrs. Barrell, also cousins, and at one time chose to consider herself engaged to one of them. To a temperament like hers the discipline of life, under such principles as governed our home, must have been severe. She was like a bird in a cage, that sometimes sings but oftener beats against the bars.*

Thus affairs went on. While the other children developed into young men and women, she felt herself passing from youth and freshness; and when, in 1806, Mr. Joseph Bray, an English gentleman, was introduced to her, she was willing to receive his admiration, and to consent to marry him. They established themselves in a house just built by Mr. Eliot, at the head of what is now Philips Place, and continued to live there till 1820, when she died, two years after the death of her husband. Faithfully did Mrs. Eliot continue the care and watchfulness she began

* I have not said enough of Fanny's fascinations and efforts to please. In person, she was pretty, *petite*, *espiègle*, had a faculty for dress and its right effect. She was fond of making presents, and gathered niceties in her chamber for *good* children; but none were admitted without invitation, and there was, perhaps, a *soupçon* of favoritism. At one time she undertook to make all the clothes for the youngest, but the little one soon outgrew her perseverance. She had good powers, and some of her faults may justly be called an inheritance. The engagement mentioned above was quite forbidden by her father, — an opposition that produced vehement excitement. When the young man died, not long after, Fanny wore mourning a long time.

on the day of her own marriage to the last hour of what became a suffering existence. Fanny was always a strong element in the family life; and care and consideration for her, which were always made duties, entered into the development of the characters of the household.

I have now come to the year 1806, when, having reached the observing age of five years, I may pretend to have personal recollections. My father was then sixty-six, full of health and activity of body and mind, attending to business, driving his horses, enjoying his friends at dinner, sometimes reading aloud in the evening. His life was so methodical and regular, that the sketch of one day would picture all the others, varied only by the change of season. He was called by one of the children at seven in summer, at eight in winter, and rose immediately. We were all expected to be ready for his summons, as soon as he came down, when he read a chapter in the Bible, and made a short and solemn prayer; a simple breakfast followed, but to this meal he never sat down; a pint bowl of milk, set aside for him the day before, with a rich cream therefore on its surface, and two or three pieces of thin toast, were all he took, and they were taken at intervals. In summer he would go into the garden, and consider its condition, or gather a flower between his draughts; in winter, examination of the hyacinths in their glasses, a visit to the book-room, or to a wood-pile admired for its exactness, filled the moment. Sometimes before this light meal was finished he was told "Mr. Mountain has come."* Mr. Mountain

* It was Mr. Eliot's fancy to have the youngest child sit upon his knee during the process of frizzing and powdering, repeating to her stories and poetry, and claiming something from the youthful memory. Mountain was a Frenchman, and, I have heard, died in an almshouse.

was a barber, according to the most familiar and accepted definition; his profession was visible in his person. Agile, courteous, plausible, and flattering, he could adapt himself to all varieties of character, and temper; — very neat, and well-mannered, always supplied with the latest news, anecdotes, and gossip, but content with silence, if that was the humor of the morning. Amiable to children, his coming was welcomed by the young ones.

At nine o'clock, Mr. Eliot went to the market, followed by the man-servant, and then to the counting-room, where, unless tempted to a drive or walk, he remained till two, the dinner-hour being half past two. After dinner he went to his "book-room" for an hour, in summer, and then followed a drive, or a lounging hour in the garden, or a visit to Mrs. Bray or to a neighbor. In winter the short afternoon was filled by a walk, and the twilight by a romp with the boys, — William, a prince of revellers, nine years old, and Sam, between six and seven, riding on his shoulders, driving him by his coat-tails, and with various other antics keeping him in full activity, and the spectators in infinite amusement. At the dark mahogany tea-table, lighted by two tall silver lamps, and brightened by the tea-kettle and various other silver articles, Mr. Eliot did sit down; but the refreshment he took was as light as at his other meals, his delicate china cup holding not more than a wine-glass, and the toast being of the thinnest. After this he lighted his Argand lamp, — a new and luxurious invention, kept in order by a daughter, being too precious to be ever trusted to a servant, — and when not inclined to read aloud, the hours till nine o'clock were passed in the book-room, with books new and old. At nine o'clock he found the same square table spread with a supper of cold meats, lobster, or a Welshrabbit, according to the season, or some little nicety from Miss Hannah's skill. This meal he enjoyed more than the others, and after his glass of old Madeira or Port, when his companions gradually left him, he sat with his book, till half past eleven or twelve, when Miss Hannah appeared to report the house closed, to receive directions, and make report of previous orders.

Such was the simple, cheerful life of these years, varied, of course, by care, regret, and pleasures. Dinner-parties were less frequent then heretofore; but the Thursday clerical dinner, with the long talk and inspiring cigar,* were still enjoyed, and visits exchanged with the Eliot, the Andrews, the Hubbard, Allen, and Cutler families, gave variety and animation.

In 1805, the family group consisted of Fanny (twenty-nine), Mary (seventeen), Eliza (fifteen), Charles (fourteen, just entered at Harvard), and four younger children, the whole group combining much variety of character and attraction, and much for discipline and help. In 1806, Fanny's marriage to Mr. Bray caused a few changes, and, by giving her a kind and judicious protector, relieved her father of some of his anxieties.

Charles's absence and exposure at such a boyish age, with an excitable and vehement nature, to the perils of a college life, created new cares and fears, mingled with satisfaction at proofs of study and good conduct. The Saturday return home and frequent drives to visit him were animating interests. Mr. Eliot often walked to see his son, when

* Mr. Eliot never used tobacco, except a rare pinch of snuff, but he was fond of the odor of cigars, and kept them for his friends.

weather and roads were favorable, for in those days the only regular communication between Boston and Cambridge was by a small coach, which made two trips a day. Everything went well with Charles, till one unlucky night, in January, 1809, when he was found with others in a classmate's room enjoying a supper of broiled chickens. A solemn example was made of these young people, by the sentence of "Suspension till Commencement."

In these days of indifference to collegiate, and to nearly all other punishments, there can be little conception of the dismay that fell upon the quiet household in Tremont Street. Mr. Eliot's displeasure and mortification were great, and so strongly expressed, that young listeners feared their brother would never recover from the disgrace.

Hampton Falls was the place designated for his banishment, and there, in the Rev. Mr. Abbott, he found so wise and kind a friend, and so good a teacher, that his heart and mind were rapidly developed, and a warm mutual attachment was formed which continued through the short life of the young student. Mr. Eliot's life was for a time saddened by this disappointment and by the recent frequent loss of near friends.

In July, 1808, Mr. and Mrs. Eliot's intimate friend and near neighbor, Mrs. Hubbard, died; in November following, Mrs. Tyng, the wife of Mrs. Eliot's only brother, was taken; and in January, 1809, came the death of Mrs. Belknap, Mr. Eliot's last sister; — a heavy series of losses in so few months. Mrs. Eliot was the tender friend of each, and was with them through their days of suffering, and in the solemn parting hours, comforting and sustaining their hearts. It might have been that the pressure of so much real sorrow would have lightened the Cambridge trouble;

but I suppose in a degree it aggravated it. Again, in February, a heavy loss fell upon Mr. Eliot, in the sudden death of Sheriff Allen, an intimate, next-door friend, for his pretty grounds, enclosing the ancient stone house, adjoined upon our garden, filling the space between that and Somerset Street. Almost daily intercourse was kept up, for, besides the friendliness between the gentlemen, Miss Patty Allen, the Sheriff's niece,* and the presiding influence in his establishment, was a great favorite with old and young. Her uncommon beauty and grace of manner were made more winning by great amiability and good sense. How well I remember the genial, jolly old Sheriff in his blue frock coat reaching to his feet, with a red collar and brass buttons, and his three-cornered hat!

In a letter to Charles, his father said: "The death of the Sheriff is a very heavy blow to me; I feel his loss very sensibly, and shall through life, as I shall never look upon his like again. Since the first of November a constant succession of sickness and death has occurred in the circle of my acquaintance. I remember not so solemn a period."

After receiving his degree at Commencement, 1809, Charles decided to study theology, and for that purpose established himself in Cambridge in November. The months of seclusion, with such influences as were gathered under Mr. Abbott's roof, had produced a great change in him. Boyishness had disappeared under the power of the collegiate punishment and the grief it had occasioned; and the generous and thoughtful elements of his character, his

* This charming vision of my youth married the son of Governor Caleb Strong, of Northampton (Governor of Massachusetts seven years, from 1800), and disappeared from amongst us, though living for some years in Boston. Such were the taste and character of Mr. Strong, that she was quite separated from those she loved.

affections, and religious feelings and principles were gradually developed and strengthened. He was fortunate in the circumstances of his second establishment in Cambridge; for, having a room adjoining one occupied by Mr. Frisbie, he found himself soon admitted to a circle embracing so much intellect, learning, elegant culture, and genial intercourse, as must have kindled in any nature some answering qualities. Charles (then nearly nineteen) had aspirations and impulses that were worthy of such influences, and his affection and reverence for Mr. Frisbie and Mr. Norton became deep and stimulating. Mr. Samuel Thacher, Mr. Buckminster, Mr. Farrar, and other intimate friends, formed a circle with powers and attractions rarely found within so narrow limits. Mr. Frisbie, with his native, gentle thoughtfulness, welcomed my brother with kindness, and, as he suffered constantly from trouble in his eyes, Charles soon became his daily companion and reader. No wonder that his father wrote thus to him soon after he was settled in Cambridge: —

"I trust in God that you are now placed in the highest and most capable situation to give you every information necessary to the accomplished scholar, and particularly fitted to classical acquirement.

"Mr. Buckminster's Phi Beta Kappa oration gives my sentiments completely on this subject. If you attempt being a scholar, be a thorough one or quit the pursuit; and let me assure you that I have a confidence that you are taking the steps I wish you to follow, that you are a student, a hard student, for labour is necessary to success.

"It is my ardent wish that you may proceed in those paths that will best conduce to the establishment of your character as a gentleman, a man of honour, the moralist, and the Christian; the last is the apex, and contains, indeed, every epithet that precedes it."

In the preceding May, Mr. Eliot had written a long letter to Charles, giving his judgment of the different professions, desiring to aid and guide, but not direct his decision. Of the law he says: "The profession of the Law I have almost deprecated for a son of mine, as one that throws wide open the door of temptation to practices of the most nefarious kind; and in the present day, when every young man almost is becoming a lawyer, in addition to the innumerable host that crowd our courts, I see not the prospect of obtaining, by honourable procedure, a comfortable subsistence." Of a physician's life he draws a most repulsive picture, but concludes, "After all, Physick is better, far better, than Law, unpalatable as it is." His sketch of the clerical profession is strong and earnest, expressing plainly his known preference for it, but imagining he conceals it. "Physick is better than Law; how infinitely better than physical are theological pursuits, adopted on principle, and pursued with vigour."

After a passage describing his high estimation of commerce, he ends his letter as follows:

"I have thus, dear Charles, in broken and hurried periods, laid before you all I can hastily collect; you must look for guidance to your Father in heaven on this all-momentous topick. Far am I from a desire of prescribing to you; I wish I had more ability to assist your resolves by rightly directing your views. I commend you to the grace and blessing of Almighty God, being

"Your anxious and affectionate Father,

"S. Eliot."

Another heavy burden upon Mr. Eliot's heart, in this trying year, was the approaching separation from his second daughter, by her marriage. Beautiful, intelligent, full of bright enthusiasm and animated interest, she gave him great happiness; and he depended upon her more than he knew, much more than he would confess. He had naturally hoped, when she married, to have her established near him; and to have a hundred rough miles placed between them seemed too hard. She was so young, too, — only twenty-one, — so ignorant of the world, so unaccustomed to care. Sheltered as she had been during all her gentle, uneventful life, how could she sustain the known and multiplied cares inevitable in so small a country town as Springfield was then? It was hard to those who knew the difficulties to think of these things, but to her, love, hope, and youth covered them with a golden cloud, which hung over reality some little time. The 19th of April, 1809, Mary married Mr. Edmund Dwight, of Springfield, and, taking her next sister, Eliza, with her, departed for her new home. The diminished circle closing behind her felt clearly how much brightness, sympathy, and support had gone from it. To the strong feelings and anxious temperament of her father, it was deeply trying, and I think that after this year of repeated separations, his spirits were never quite so bright. The condition of Europe oppressed his thoughts; he followed the course of affairs in France, the increase of Napoleon's power, and the state of parties in England with anxious eagerness; felt sure that nothing could resist the Corsican, — that when he had subdued Europe, America would succumb easily; and he would say to Mrs. Eliot, "Make up your mind to it: you will one day have a French *gendarme* sitting by your fire, watching your daughters, and insulting everybody." In some things his vivid imagination was his greatest enemy.

In October, 1810, our much-loved and sincerely respected grandmother, Mrs. Atkins, died,—a loss felt widely, and, in our circle, very deeply. To have so much religious wisdom, such a constant teaching of faithfulness, patient cheerfulness, and gentle courtesy taken from us,—to lose such animated affection, such unfailing sympathy for all ages and all conditions, was a trial, even for the youngest. Her age was great, and the last years had brought suffering from gout, and a degree of helplessness; but a clear mind, deep affections, and cheerful resignation sustained her through life to her last moments. It was said of her by one who knew her well, "The excellence which others attain to in the theory of virtue and religion she made the familiar practice of her life; the knowledge for which some depend on books seemed in her the result of a superior mind, exercised on its own reflections and observations; or rather she possessed the admirable talent of so blending it with the dictates of her own judgment and experience as to give it the impress of wisdom." I find a letter from my father to my sister Mary, announcing this ending of a Christian life.

"*To Mrs. Mary H. Dwight, Springfield.*

"BOSTON, October 17, 1810.

"DEAR MARY,— . . . . At half an hour past seven o'clock last evening your grandmother breathed her last, in the most tranquil and quiet manner, without a groan or sigh. Thus has she ended a long life, and left us to pray to God that our last end may be like hers, at the same time remembering (and deeply may the all-important truth be impressed on our hearts) that we may not expect that our lot and portion shall be with the righteous unless our lives are conformed to theirs, and to the infinitely greater example of the Author and Finisher of our faith. . . . .

"Such a friend as your grandmother should survive in our memories as a monitor, to guide and govern our conduct, and regulate all our actions. The example of the virtuous and the good should have, and, if properly attended to, will have, a great effect. Your grandmother was furnished by nature, or rather by the God of nature, with a mind and ability of considerable strength. She was a lady of appearance and manner that excited attention, and commanded respect; she was amiable, social, prudent, wise, honourable, virtuous, benevolent, humble, and religious. If this is true, and true it is, shall we deeply mourn her departure? when, more especially, it is said, 'Blessed are the dead who die in the Lord'; and further still, when she had been so long continued, and her faculties remained little impaired to the last? How much better than to have her live a burthen to herself and a grief to her dearest connections!

"Mr. Cary* told her, when he came to see her [in her last hours], that he came to congratulate her; and well he

* The Rev. Samuel Cary, of the Stone Chapel, Boston, son of Dr. Cary, of Newbury. Mrs. Atkins was much attached to this excellent young man, who had been much in her family, and was treated by her as if he were one of her own. On the occasion referred to, he said to Mrs. Atkins, with animation, "Grandmother, I have come to rejoice with you!" She answered, "I have finished my course, I have kept the faith; henceforth there is laid up for me a crown of righteousness, which God, the righteous Judge, shall give me in that day." "Grandmother, you are going to be very happy, where you will meet Dr. Bass, my father, and all your friends." She laid her hand upon his head, and said, "God bless you! you are a dear boy." He knelt by her and prayed most devoutly and tenderly.

might. He asked leave to pray with her, — more, I am told, a prayer of thanksgiving than of supplication.

"And now, my dear child, what should be the conclusion of this matter? I say unto you, and say solemnly, 'Go thou and do likewise'; and recollect the increased fault, nay, crime, if, with so near and dear an example before you, you fall short of her virtues.

". . . . I have written this under circumstances very unpropitious to writing, with a troubled and distracted mind, and with the children around me. I saw Mr. Cutter before I quitted Newbury at ten this morning. He will do what little is to be done; every arrangement is committed to his care, — the funeral proposed for Friday or Saturday. Your uncle Tyng is at Plymouth, expected home to-morrow. How is Mr. Dwight? how is the child? and how are you?

"Your affectionate Father,

"S. Eliot."

"*To Mrs. Dwight.*

"Boston, 16 September, 1812.

". . . . Knowing as I do the perpetual and never-to-be satisfied expectations of some of your friends, of an uninterrupted, unintermitted course and intercourse, of change and interchange of letters, — letters upon letters, — now a page or two, and now two or three sheets, — why, I really begin to pity you, and am by humane feelings almost led to think that my expectation of hearing from you, and being indulged with the high effusions of your pen, must be circumscribed indeed. The flight of letters may, for a time, do well enough for young misses, who love to indulge in the romance too incident to eternal letter-writing;

but this cannot be expected, or ought not to be of such a settled, staid, sober, and discreet matron as you.

" . . . . I hope, madam, that you duly noted, and properly appreciated, my very good-natured, cheerful, prompt consent to your mother's visit to Springfield, and even my ready consent to an extension of the time she had herself proposed as the limit of her time with you. I think in this solitary instance, at least, I bore my severe sufferings with some grace.

" . . . . Walking in the garden on a Sunday evening, during your mother's absence, it popped into my head that I would attempt a little rhyme or doggerel, partly to see how far my powers had declined from their former *flatness*, fearing they might have become a little *steep*. . . . .

" *To my Wife.*

" Absence from you is still my dread,
For whilst the path of life I tread,
My temporal joys depend on you.
What is the worth of honors, wealth,
What are good spirits, and firm health,
Unless your presence crowns my view ?

" The choicest wines, the cheerful friend,
A short, a meteor's gleam may lend ;
But clouds and darkness must ensue,
If absent from my joy in you.

" Poets in fiction best succeed,
So say a false, misjudging, breed,
Whose hearts love's fires ne'er could melt,
Who ne'er the tender passion felt.
Such I exclude, to those appeal
Who have the godlike power to feel
The wound that absence sure must give
To those who in each other live !

"Come then, return, restore to life!
Can I exist without my wife?
Behold she comes! Be still, my fears, —
All nature blooms when she appears;
Hope, joy, and bliss diffuse around,
And common soil turns Eden's ground.

"This is the only copy, and you will put it in the fire. How my spirits can carry me into the region of tolerable cheerfulness is a little mysterious even to myself, though your sister Bray has done me the justice to say she thinks I support myself wonderfully well, — sadly low at times, however. Eliza is at Hingham, William at Blue Hills. I hear with pleasure that we are soon to see you with the children.

"Your affectionate Father,

"S. Eliot."

Thus the years passed on, leaving strong effects upon young and old: old friends passed away, young ones advanced, and grandchildren brought new life to the home.

Time and changes had naturally a little impaired the elasticity of spirits for which Mr. Eliot had been remarkable, and he allowed his imagination to be more colored by fear than by hope. He was now seventy years old, and needed quiet and cheerful influences about him. He had them in larger measure than he realized, and he was to have bitter teaching, by deprivation of some that he possessed.

Charles, in three years of study, had developed a strong character, acquired learning, and shown powers of usefulness, and a desire for it, that made one who knew him more thoroughly than any friend beyond his family, and who loved him truly, — Mr. Norton, — say of him, "If he had lived to take that station for which he seemed destined, he would have been one of those who give its character to society, who guide and direct public opinion and feeling."

While so faithfully preparing for future duties, and gathering strength to help others through the perils of life, he was active and influential in forming the plan of theological studies at Cambridge "whose advantages have since been experienced"; "he suggested and promoted the Cambridge edition of Schleusner's Lexicon, and wrote the principal part of its prospectus"; and he aided largely in the publication and support of the Cambridge General Repository, of which Mr. Norton was editor, besides contributing to it with his pen. In January, 1813 (when twenty-one), he was examined and approved by the Boston Association of Clergymen, and soon after preached his first sermon at Dr. Pierce's church in Brookline. His second was at the church of his venerable kinsman, Dr. John Eliot. I suppose that the human heart is hardly capable of a deeper happiness than Mr. Eliot felt when hearing his son deliver from the pulpit the well-considered, well-expressed thought which marks his writings, with a calm and solemn manner, proving entire sincerity and devotion. He pleased and attracted without dazzling; it was his subject, and not his own thoughts, that occupied him; while his pale, intellectual face and tall, fragile form added interest to his words. I find but one allusion to this most interesting occasion, — in a letter from Mrs. Eliot to her sister, Miss Atkins, written the 12th of March. "You say I have not told you how I like Charles as a preacher. I can give a good reason: I *do not know*. To pretend to give an opinion from the opportunity I have had to judge, would be rash indeed. I could not form anything like a correct opinion of his manner, for I could not venture to look at him enough; I have read two of his sermons, that I think very good, and I hear he is well spoken of. I have no doubt his talents are good. His application has been great, and, if his health is preserved, I think his love of study will make him capable of usefulness." How restrained and tremulous was the mother's joy! Fear hung about her heart.

Once more Charles preached, — in Mr. Lowell's church, where his boyhood had been taught, and where familiar faces met his eye, — and then his rich, sweet voice was heard no more in public. A cold, a cough, prostration, the aggravating power of the chill of spring, — how well the course is known!

In the early summer he returned to his father's house, a conqueror, yet overcome, — a patient sufferer. The progress of the disease was rapid; he had taxed mind and body so fully that the end of power was approaching. Strength failed gradually, but not his acquiescence; he taught resignation to all who came near him. His faithful and tender friend, Mr. Norton, thus writes of him: —

"There are few spectacles of higher moral sublimity than to see one to whom the future promised so much calmly, and without perturbation, waiting the slow approach of death, with a knowledge of its certainty, and a full apprehension of all that we can know of its nature. This was done by Mr. Eliot. . . . . He spoke, as he had done in health, of his trust in the mercy and providence of God, and of his belief of the high destination of those who endeavor to fulfil the purposes of their existence. It produced a feeling almost of cheerfulness to hear him talk of death, and of his hope of meeting again the friends who had gone before him from this world."

Truly the hand of God was heavy upon Mr. Eliot, and well did Charles understand what he suffered, not only from the crushing of his hopes, but the thought that one so young, so fit to help and elevate other lives, to be the staff and support of his own old age, must pass through this portal of bitter suffering, and depart. Charles strove to lead him to acquiesce and let him go when his Heavenly Father called him, without repining; and it was pitiful and touching to see the effort each made to cheer the other, in the father's visits to his son's chamber. He could command himself but for a short time, and with a wrung heart would hasten to the garden, and there walk up and down with heavy groans. The summer days and weeks passed on; the deep pathos, the tender ministrations, the hush of the house, grew hour by hour. Mother, sisters, brothers, and friends gathered where the young disciple was submissively laying down his life, at the moment when labor seemed about to be recompensed and hopes fulfilled. His temperament was vehement and impulsive, his human ambition and desire to gratify the hopes and wishes of his parents must have been very strong, his physical sufferings were severe; but he had so overcome himself and the world, through deep religious faith and entire trust in God, that quiet and calmness rested upon his spirit. He received his friends with cheerfulness and interest, and tried to induce all who approached him to gain the faith that supported him.

I give a short letter from Mrs. Eliot written at this time.

"August 14, 1813.

"I wish it was in my power to give my dear sisters a full view of my mind at this moment. I am generally tranquil, seldom much distressed. I may be called to harder trials than I now endure. If thus it is to be, I will hope that my strength will be proportioned, that I may at all times give thanks to the Father of mercies, who has, in so many instances, blessed me, and who now has mixed so many comforts in my cup. Although it is a bitter draught, I feel that mercy and goodness have called me to drink it. I cannot refuse it; I will not murmur, but say 'Thy will be done,' for it is good.

"I am truly, your affectionate Sister,

"C. Eliot."

A few weeks more, and the closing scene came; the earthly life of that pure spirit ended the 28th September, and never shall I forget the pitiful sight of his father's tottering steps as, leaning upon William's arm, he followed* all that was left of long cherished hope to the tomb. The heavy hand of grief bent his head and shook his vigorous frame; he was burying desires, affections, ambitions, that were a part of his vitality. For a time he could not be comforted, yet he strove to submit. He longed for sympathy, but was overcome by any expression of it, and fled to the solitude of his room. I have found only two written expressions of his feelings.

* It was the custom at that time for gentlemen, relatives and friends, to follow the hearse on foot in the centre of the street, forming sometimes a long procession. Ladies, who previously had also walked, now went in carriages.

"*To the Rev. Charles Lowell.*

"Boston, December 15, 1813.

"My dear Sir, — The early and strong interest you took in the reputation, credit, and advancement of my departed son, and the publick honours you have paid him, demand all the gratitude that a heart of the strongest sensibility could feel; and it is with eyes suffused with tears that I offer you the tribute of my thanks.

"I have particularly noted and deeply felt the last instance of your unremitted endeavours to console and support me by the loan of the Life of the Son of Dr. Beattie, and the hour of its communication could not miss my grateful remark.

"I have suffered much in reading it, and by several late concurring circumstances, though in sacred silence, not a word having passed my lips. I would bow with submission to the will of God; and remember that 'Suffering refines, exalts the soul, Suffering is virtue's highest school.'

"I do not wish to escape it; I only pray to God to enable me to bear his corrections with a proper temper and disposition, and to reward you for all your labours of love and kind attentions to

"Your deeply afflicted and obliged Friend,

"S. Eliot."

"*Written on the Death of a Son.*

"Behold, O God, my sorrowing heart,
By mournful scenes distress'd,
Call'd by thy providence to part
With what I thought my rest!

"When all my fondest wishes seem'd
 Approaching to their goal,
And pleas'd anticipation deem'd
 I had attained the whole.

"Ah! when to my enraptur'd view
 My hopes were chang'd to joy,
'T was then fear, death, my mind subdue,
 And my best plans destroy!

"The object who so long had been
 The care of every hour
Faints, sickens, dies! Support me then,
 O Thou who hast the power!

"Such is the lot of hapless man, —
 To-day we spring and bloom,
To-morrow's different page we scan,
 And drop into the tomb!

"Help me to see this dread event
 An act of love divine,
And know thy sharpest lessons sent
 T' amend, exalt, refine!

"Teach me submission to thy will,
 And may I kiss the rod;
May my few days each duty fill,
 And wing my way to God!

"August 28, 1814."

It was in the year 1814 that Mr. Eliot, with the assistance of Mr. John Lowell, a faithful friend and much-prized companion, established the Greek Professorship at Cambridge; but nothing was known to *any one* but Mr. Lowell of his being the founder, till after his death in 1820. Mr. Quincy, in his History of Harvard University, says, 'The donation bestowed by Samuel Eliot ($ 20,000), in the foundation of the Greek Professorship, was the largest sum ever bestowed on the college by any benefactor in his lifetime, and the interest received before his death was equivalent to an addition of eight thousand dollars to the original gift. The bounty of no individual flowed from a higher or a purer source. It was unsolicited and unavowed. It had its origin in the recesses of his powerful mind. . . . .

" In the life of Samuel Eliot, charity went hand in hand with success. As a merchant he was prosperous and without reproach. Amid the active pursuits of business he cultivated a taste for literature and the arts; to the severity of ancient morals he united the faith of a liberal Christian, and joined a thorough knowledge of the world with a predilection for retirement and domestic life."

Of course, in the complete ignorance of the family as to the giver of this liberal donation, the news was received as of any other agreeable public fact and individual generosity. I have no recollection or association with it. My father, behind the shield of secrecy so faithfully held before him by Mr. Lowell, must have had some enjoyment in hearing it discussed and praised, and used skill in taking or avoiding a share in the comments. He was very anxious as to who should be appointed as Professor, having a strong wish that Mr. Norton should be chosen, and was much disappointed, almost displeased, when Mr. Everett was selected, February, 1815. Mr. Everett was inaugurated in April, but, as he passed the next four years in Europe, he did not enter upon his duties till 1819. He had been the clergyman of the Brattle Street Church for two years, and was distinguished by his brilliant talents and great popularity in society. Mr. Eliot had very little personal knowledge of him, and was not prepossessed in his favor. It was, therefore, a double disappointment, and without doubt it was aggravated by the long delay of the instruction he had provided for.

The days and months as they passed were heavy with sadness to Mr. Eliot's heart. He was now seventy-four, and most of his friends and contemporaries had passed away. One who had been taken in February, 1813, — Dr. John Eliot, — was a near relative and life-long friend, who was always ready with sympathy and gentle and wise influences, and who would have been a strong support in these bitter hours of bereavement. The last time he was in his pulpit was when his young kinsman spoke to his people, preparing to take up the duties and offices so faithfully filled by the venerable listener. In a few months both were released from earthly burdens. Much was his kindly and strengthening companionship missed by Mr. and Mrs. Eliot.

The regular routine of life continued. Mr. Eliot went to his counting-room every morning, but attended to no business, except what the care of his property forced upon him. He strove to read, but books rarely fixed his attention, and he would sit for hours, his head resting on his hand, or walk back and forth in the garden or the parlor. But as the winter advanced he found occupation and a mournful interest, in selecting and arranging, with the help of Mr. Norton,* a collection of Charles's Essays and Ser-

* Mr. Eliot frequently walked to and from Cambridge when desiring Mr. Norton's advice and help.

mons. It was printed, not published, but the interest it excited was a soothing gratification to the parents who had seen so much fade from life.

Peace with England brightened all hearts in the spring, and daily life brought many sources of interest and cheerfulness to those who sat in the shadow of sorrow. William had done well through his whole college life, and when he graduated, in August, 1815, had the Latin Poem assigned to him by the government of the college. It gratified his father, who partly to please his son, and partly as a compliment to the college, determined to give an entertainment in Cambridge on Commencement-day, like many that had been given on the same occasion, though on a different scale. There was generally a gathering of friends and strangers at a collation, immediately after the performances of the young men had ended; and as there was no suitable hall in Cambridge for the purpose, it had been once or twice held in a marquee.

Mr. Eliot's invitations included all his acquaintance in the country, as well as town, and all the strangers who, at that period, were attracted to the Cambridge Commencement in great numbers. Applications for invitations were freely made for the friends of friends, and freely given; till more than five hundred citizens, good and true, were summoned.

There was much occupation, bustle, and excitement in the quiet household, suddenly taken from the closest seclusion and brought into contact with hosts of advisers, helpers, and providers; for the resources for such occasions in 1815 bore no proportion to those of the present day. The landlord of the Exchange Hotel, in Boston, was to send out the materials for the collation, and his limited experience in such affairs needed much aid. A house was hired for the reception of the guests, rooms being arranged for refreshing the gay summer toilets of the ladies; an immense marquee was raised in a field opposite; a band of music cheered the spirits of the company, and, after the collation and the coffee, the younger portion of the company were indulged in a little dancing on the green in front of the house. All was gayety, animation, and propriety; there were no visible *contretemps*, and before the summer twilight had passed away the crowd had dispersed, the heroes and heroines of the day, the lovers and the flirters, no doubt lamenting that such bright hours must end. It was a wonderful episode in the secluded life in Tremont Street, but tranquillity and retirement soon again encircled the household. William, with his gay, fresh, contagious spirits (his heart already in the keeping of another), established himself for serious work in Mr. William Prescott's office, and added greatly to the cheerfulness of the home.

Mrs. Dwight returned this season to her native town, and established herself in a house where the Athenæum now stands; and her unchanged brightness and intelligence, and her little ones, were sources of constant interest and refreshment.

Mrs. Searle, Mrs. Eliot's oldest sister, had been living with her family for a year or two in one of Mr. Eliot's houses, next his own (where now stands the Pavilion Hotel), and with her uncommon strength of mind, quiet dignity, and warm affections, was a strengthening and cheering influence to all, and a great happiness to Mrs. Eliot.

Mr. Eliot's spirits, though variable, had brightened in the last months, and his health remained vigorous; but as the winter of 1815-16 advanced, a new cloud seemed settling upon him, too dark for concealment, but never explained. He went to his counting-room as usual, and to his book-room in the evenings, but he came from both in deep depression. No one could detect the cause. At length he brought home one day the morning paper, and, to the astonishment of all, permitted his daughter to read to him certain portions of it. It was usually the earliest interest of the day, and why he submitted to hearing it read, was a question which filled the minds of the household.

It continued to be the occupation of the afternoon, while silent unhappiness increased. His habits and movements appeared the same as usual till late in the winter, when, coming home at noon one day, he found it difficult to guide himself through the streets. Then, for the first time, he told Mrs. Eliot that for many months cataracts had been forming upon both his eyes. It was mournful news, and we wondered not only how he had so silently endured so great a trouble, but how he would be able to support what must follow.

Few persons, I imagine, were ever more determined, both from preference and from principle, to be absolutely independent of the services of others, personally, and in all affairs of business or care of property. He chose to manage and direct what belonged to him, without advice or intervention. He really disliked hearing others read. What hidden struggles and strong trouble he must have passed through, as darkness gradually thickened upon him, and the conviction that he must rely upon others for everything grew more decided! He went no more into the street, but a rope stretched along the garden path, at the height of his hand, afforded means for taking air and exercise. Reading became his only solace, but at great cost of patience and taste. Many voices were at his command. Through courtesy some kind offers were accepted; but the manner so often clouded the matter and diminished the pleasure, that it soon became the habit for the two youngest daughters to devote alternate days wholly to his service. He was thus free to correct emphasis, pronunciation, or too great rapidity, to interrupt at his pleasure, and to break the reading by dictating letters or notes. This last occupation quickened his interest and animation. He was generally very patient.

By degrees the readers became better able to suit the sensitive ear and refined taste, and to continue the occupation through eight hours, in the divisions of morning, afternoon, and evening. With an acceptable book and a contented listener, the work was easy; but at all times the entrance of a visitor who was welcome to the recluse was cheering to the reader.

It was difficult in those days, as in all others, to find a succession of books that could stand the test of being read aloud. There were few private libraries, and the one or two Circulating Libraries contained little but trash. Histories and works in many volumes Mr. Eliot did not enjoy. Reviews and magazines afforded amusement, but they were few in number at that time. The advent of Campbell's "Specimens of the British Poets" made an epoch of refreshment and delight, and Miss Edgeworth's and the Waverley Novels, as they came in succession, were hailed like personal benefactors.

But with all help and kindness, all efforts for resignation, and all hopes of future relief, the days and months wore on heavily. Even after so long a life of labor and care, of excitement, sorrow, and disappointment, such enforced quiet, and rest, were not welcome. He was imprisoned with backward-looking thoughts, and he would gladly have sought relief from them in the activity that still seemed possible, with such clearness of mind, and vigor of body as he possessed. But as I recall his bearing under these trials of his temperament and character, I perceive that he maintained the same resolute strength, and the same firm principles, that had sustained him through life.

After many consultations and discussions, Mr. Eliot determined to have an operation performed upon his eyes, in the spring of 1817, by Mr. Nathan Smith, of Hanover, New Hampshire, a distinguished surgeon and oculist. He was a man of genius in his profession, with a full and ready mind, quick wit, and most genial humor, and during the six weeks that he was an inmate of Mr. Eliot's home, his cheerfulness, unfailing fund of anecdote and story, his kindliness and strong sense brightened many hours. He was summoned to many other patients at various distances, but made Mr. Eliot his first care.

The operation was skilfully performed, but the cataracts were soft, and the absorption necessary to a cure was a strong test of the vigor of the eyes and of the general health. It was an anxious interval, and the question whether his great age would prevent recovery — whether he was to be a prisoner in darkness the rest of his life or be freed for new enjoyment — made all anxious who surrounded him. When the time came to test the result, and the bandages were removed, he saw, and great was the excitement and joy. Great care and restriction were indispensable, but constant experiments and measurements of the amount of sight were made; and so much was recovered before the autumn that he could read a little could go about freely, and was full of hope and content. But one day, in too full confidence of strength, he read a whole paper in his favorite book, — the Rambler, —and inflammation immediately followed. It was an acute disappointment, and the winter was a dreary season of alternating hope and discouragement, as the inflammation lessened and returned. Much sympathy, constant kind attention from friends, and the devotion of the family, gave what alleviation was possible; but it could be only alleviation. Submission was difficult.

In March, 1817, my sister Eliza's marriage to Mr. Guild gave an added friend to the circle, always ready for any kindness or service, and as both Mary and Eliza were then established in houses next to Mrs. Bray's, we felt surrounded by affection and sympathy. Sam, too, having graduated in the autumn, was more at home, and free to devote himself to his father; and William, the young law student was always ready with his pen or supporting arm; but he never could make his reading acceptable to the sensitive ear. His bright mind, ready wit, and quick feeling, his beautiful singing and his frolics, were infinite refreshments to the rest of the household, in the intervals of his studies and engagements. In the spring of 1818 his engagement to Miss Bradford seemed to fill the measure of his happiness, and of his resolution to deserve it. In the following summer he sailed for England, having determined to pursue his law studies in London for at least one season. This was a gratification to Mr. Eliot, who always held the faith that the best of everything, whether intellectual or material, was only to be obtained in that glorious island. But the place so filled by William could be supplied by no one else; stillness and gravity settled more and more upon the circle.

Frequent inflammations and returning dimness of the sight, seemed only preludes to entire blindness. Dr. Smith offered some hope from a second operation, and it was performed in September, 1818. It produced very little effect, but it was final; restless anxiety, agitating hopes, and eager grasping after remedies were quieted, and resignation to the inevitable, grew to calmness. Old habits and resources were gathered up, and the days slipped away peacefully.

Mr. Eliot declined to see strangers; his great age—he was now seventy-nine—and oppressed spirits were natural objections, but he had also an unacknowledged feeling of mortification at his helplessness. He had reached the period when the heart and thoughts of men, weary with the cares and burdens of life, most need the cheering faces of friends, and the light and power of the sun. His strong sense of beauty,* his delight in nature, from a broad landscape to the most delicate flower, his pleasure in animals, from a fine horse to the birds that clustered in his garden and the kitten that so often followed his steps or climbed to his shoulder, must have supplied and brightened his reveries, but no doubt sharpened his sense of loss. Still he bore himself with a firmness and patience, that astonished even those who knew him best.

Rather absorbed by my recollections of this particular trial, I have not noted in its place a sudden sorrow that

* One of my cousins, who remembers my father longer than I can, speaks of her strong impression of his delicate feeling, and his enjoyment of all beauty, particularly the loveliness of children. She recalls, with much feeling, his tenderness and consideration through the illness and death of one of her sisters at his house. Mr. Eliot shrank from the sight of suffering and acute sorrow, it almost unmanned him; "but when their presence was inevitable, nothing could exceed his kindness."

came upon us in February, 1818. Mr. Bray, in walking through a narrow passage on his way home one evening, in a blinding snow-storm, struck his head against an iron bar, and soon after was seized with apoplexy. He never recovered consciousness, and died in five days. It was a sad event to us all. His perfect temper and equability, his truthfulness and sincere kindness, had won true respect and affection, and from Mr. Eliot, in his state of dependence, it took a long-trusted support, and renewed the sharp anxiety of early years for the bereaved wife. She gave herself up to grief, never left her house, and demanded constant care and companionship. Her father went to her often, making pathetic efforts to forget his own loss and burdens, for her sake.

I think it was in this winter that the oldest daughter of his sister, Mrs. Belknap, died, calling forth from Mrs. Eliot that tender sympathy, presence of mind, and wise action so often shown before.

Another year passed away in quiet patience. Little Catherine Dwight, then two years old, was a daily pleasure to her grandfather, coming to him every morning after her breakfast, and, with her sweet voice, imperfect words, and caressing ways, charming him, as her lovely color, her brown curls, and pretty figure delighted those whose senses were more complete She came dancing in with the reigning favorite book or toy, and would sit on her grandfather's knee through the operations of the *friseur*, reciting most dramatically verses or stories, and often attracting admirers from both sections of the family. What a bright vision she was! — animated and gay, yet gentle and docile; affectionate, full of intelligence and quick perception, her intelligent remarks and questions enchanted the aged

how they ought to treat it—that they ought to read it *daily*, *attentively*, *devoutly*, and *perseveringly*, and that when they understand its directions, without delay and without ceasing, they must follow them. He may then show the benefits, for time and eternity, of thus studying the Bible; and may offer to assist all among his beloved people who wish to enter upon the study of it, in a Bible-class."

Suggestions are then given as to forming the class; various ways in which the minister may assist them to a right understanding of the Scriptures; with specimens of proper questions and answers on select portions of the Bible, and explanations of the topics suggested, which the minister may give. "And let the members of the class commence with a fixed purpose, trusting in Jesus Christ alone, to ask of God daily to teach them his will; and daily to listen to his voice speaking to them in his word, that they may understand it. And when they do understand it, let nothing hinder them from doing it, for the purpose of glorifying God, becoming in temper like him, and performing his will. They will then find that the Bible is perfect, converting the soul; sure, making wise the simple; right, rejoicing the heart; pure, enlightening the eyes; true and righteous altogether; more to be desired than gold, yea, than much fine gold; and that in obeying it there is indeed a great reward."

March 19, 1826, he preached to his own people a most effective sermon, which was then printed, and immediately after embodied in the series of the Amer-

but little, continuing almost his usual habits till, in the last days of the fortnight, he grew more tranquil, perhaps more feeble, and consented to remain in his chamber. It was on the 18th of January, while my sister Catherine was alone with him, that he tranquilly and almost instantly passed from one life to another. All who were in the house were gathered about him in a moment, physicians were called, and hurried efforts made to recall life; but the great change, the great release had come, the spirit had parted from its companion and interpreter during eighty years, had escaped from that narrow, darkened dwelling, and reached new sight and fresh existence. It was a peaceful end of a long and rich experience.

I have sketched a simple, unpretending life, in no way remarkable for uncommon talent, or for rare events, but dignified by unfaltering uprightness, high aims, and steadfast resolution. With nothing to rely upon in youth and manhood but personal industry, self-denial, and determined adherence to truth and honesty through all temptations, he gained not only friends, wealth, and an honored position in the community, but opportunity to serve that community, and to leave a record of noble liberality. His mode of life was modest and retiring; his strong desire was to enlarge his own mind, and to help and stimulate others to do the same. He governed his household and educated his children by the best light and knowledge he possessed; he was a sincere and constant friend, and kind and generous to those whom he found struggling as he had done. There was nobleness in his nature, his impulses were generous, his sensibilities quick and tender;

suddenly excited feeling sometimes made him unjust, or strengthened a prejudice, but self-command and regret soon followed.

Among my strongest impressions of my father are those of his firmness and refinement. Whatever his principles or his intellect suggested should be done, he found means to accomplish. Though bred in poverty, and knowing but short intervals from hard work in manhood, his manners expressed self-respect, a courtly desire to please, and a refined decision, that compelled consideration and good manners from others. His style of living, the occupations of his leisure, expressed a sound judgment and a fine natural taste. Neither elation nor ostentation were seen in him; he did not conceal the humble beginning of his life, nor did he disparage its subsequent success.

Integrity, faithfulness, obedience to the laws of God and of conscience, were the rules of his life. He has left to his descendants an example that, faithfully followed, will not only be an honor to him, but bring rich blessings upon them.

ADDITIONAL PAPERS.

ADDITIONAL PAPERS.

SOON after Mr. Eliot's death it was announced to his family, by Mr. John Lowell, that he was the founder of the Greek Professorship at Cambridge University, — a fact so faithfully kept secret for six years that it excited almost as much surprise as pleasure. The Corporation of the College sent, through a committee, a letter to the family, expressing "their sense of the liberality and importance of the benefaction, the obligations of the University to the author of this act of munificence, and their condolence at the loss they had sustained."

The many princely gifts to public institutions in late years make this endowment appear a modest one, but in 1814 it was widely noticed and cordially praised.

Extracts from a letter from the Hon. John Lowell to Mr. William H. Eliot, then in Europe.

"BOSTON, February 4, 1820.

"DEAR SIR, — You will probably have heard before the present letter will reach you (for what has swifter wings than calamity?) of the departure of your father, and my excellent and constant friend. It seems to me impossible that both at the moment of your quitting him, and whenever you turned your thoughts homeward, it should not have been contemplated as an event of not improbable occurrence. For the strength and vigor of his constitution, at his advanced age, must have appeared to you, as to others, as a protracted miracle, out of the course of nature, and therefore that when the thread should break, it would snap suddenly.

"These anticipations, I know, often took firm hold of his own mind, and never were they so distinctly expressed to me as when he was called upon to bid you adieu. He had a prophetic feeling that it was the last glance he should ever cast upon his son. . . . .

"I wish you had been at home to receive the consolation under this bereavement, to have your share of the melancholy pleasure, derived from the unanimous testimony of the wise and good to the excellence of his character, — from the praise — just praise — bestowed upon him for his munificence, beneficence, and magnanimity, and a praise scarcely inferior for his judgment and excellent discrimination in the apportionment of his estate among his family. A most distinguished law character assured me that he esteemed it the most honorable testament ever made in the United States, — a perpetual lesson which would be invaluable as an example, — adding that several opulent men had declared their intention to procure an office copy of it as a model. This is just. Such a testament is far more influential than the most touching, heart-rending discourse of Massillon, Saurin, or Taylor. Men who can withstand eloquence, and the reproaches of conscience, are often unable to resist the strong influence of an undivided public sentiment.

"Already I have perceived in many rich men a sort of *posthumous sensibility;* they begin to ask, what will the world say of me and my testament when it comes to pronounce its last and loud sentence on my memory? God intended this public sentiment as one of the restraints on immoral or dishonorable conduct. . . . .

"That your journey may have been as productive of pleasure, as improving to your mind, and as rich a source of future agreeable recollections as you could wish, and that you may be restored to those who love you, and whom you love, improved in health, and to taste pleasures which Europe with all her stores can never furnish, is the sincerest wish of your father's closest friend, and one who would fain be esteemed yours,

"John Lowell."

www.ingramcontent.com/pod-product-compliance
Lightning Source LLC
LaVergne TN
LVHW011212110826
845150LV00006B/1410

* 9 7 8 1 4 2 5 5 1 7 4 1 0 *